trellises
and ARBORS

By Kenneth S. Burton, Jr. and the Editors of Sunset Books, Menlo Park, California

Cover: An elegant white arbor spans a narrow walkway (see page 96). Arbor design by Freeland Tanner. Cover design by Vasken Guiragossian. Photography by Saxon Holt.

PHOTOGRAPHERS **Scott Atkinson:** 19 bottom, 113; **Gay Bumgarner:** 80; **Karen Bussolini:** 8, 13 top right, 19 top, 45 top; **Rob Cardillo:** 9 right; **Ken Chen:** 88 bottom; **Claire Curran:** 36; **R. Todd Davis:** 16 bottom, 18 bottom right, 27 top left; **Richard Day/Daybreak Imagery:** 18 bottom left; **Susan Day/Daybreak Imagery:** 52; **Ken Druse:** 7; **Laura Dunkin-Hubby:** 46 all except top left; **Catriona Tudor Erler:** 10 bottom, 17 top, 35 top left, 62 bottom, 102; **Derek Fell:** 10 top, 22 top; **Roger Foley:** 1, 38, 39 all, 43 all, 47, 50–51 all, 56–57 all, 59 all, 65 all, 71 all, 74, 76–77 all, 82–83 all, 86–87 all, 92–95 all, 100–101 all, 104–107 all, 110–112 all, 116–117 all; **John Glover:** 6 top right, 11 bottom right, 13 bottom right, 27 right, 35 bottom, 64; **Jay Graham:** 97 top; **Jerry Harpur:** 34 top; **Lynne Harrison:** 23 bottom, 27 bottom left, 60; **Philip Harvey:** 46, 55 top; **Saxon Holt:** 22 bottom, 29 top, 67 bottom, 69, 96, 122 top right; **Dency Kane:** 34 bottom; **Lynn Karlin:** 14 left and top right, 35 top right, 40, 44, 63 top, 68 top, 70, 97 bottom; **Dennis Krukowski:** 12 top left, 20 top right, 32 top; **Janet Loughrey:** 23 top; **Allan Mandell:** 24 both, 61, 84, 88 top, 108; **Charles Mann:** 21 bottom, 29 bottom, 128; **M.A.P./F. Buffetrille:** 6 left; **M.A.P./A. Descat:** 11 top; **M.A.P./N. & P. Mioulane:** 31 both, 114; **M.A.P./F. Strauss:** 63 bottom; **E. Andrew McKinney:** 46 top left; **Emily Minton:** 26; **Jerry Pavia:** 14 bottom right, 28 top, 29 center left, 42, 45 bottom, 54, 62 top, 118–121 all, 122 bottom left, 123–127 all; **Norman A. Plate:** 13 left, 53 bottom, 55 center and bottom, 66, 89 all; **Robert Perron:** 41 bottom, 79; **Cheryl R. Richter:** 98; **Richard Shiell:** 17 bottom; **Pam Spaulding:** 53 top; **Tim Street-Porter:** 20 left; **Nance S. Trueworthy:** 90; **Mark Turner:** 15, 28 bottom, 41 top, 58; **Brian Vanden Brink:** 4, 6 bottom right, 12 bottom left, 25, 30 both, 32 bottom, 33, 72; **Deidra Walpole:** 2 right, 9 top and bottom left, 16 top, 18 top, 21 top left and right, 29 bottom right, 67 top, 68 bottom; **Judy White/GardenPhotos.com:** 11 bottom left, 48; **Martha Woodward:** 122 bottom right

DESIGNERS/GARDENS **7** Design: Ken Druse **8** New York Botanical Garden **9 top left** Design: Edith Malek; **right** Design: Barbara Ellis; **bottom left** Design: Edith Malek **12 top left** Design: Brian J. Koribanick, Landscape Techniques, Inc. **14 bottom right** Design: Sharon Drusch **15** Design: Larry and Stephanie Feeney **16 top** Rohman garden **18 top** McGovern garden **19 top** Design: Sundial Herb Garden; **bottom** Design: Mary Gordon, Ruth Gordon, and Francisco Alfonso **20 top right** Landscape design: Katie Brown; **left** Artist/designer: Nancy Kintish **21 top right** Ferrare garden; **top left** Sharon Milder garden; **bottom** Design: Sally Robertson **24 bottom** Design: Scott Kesterson; Garden design: Linda Ernst **26** Landscape architect: Blayney Fox Myers **27 right** Design: Chris Jacobsen **28 bottom** Bellevue Botanical Garden **29 top** Design: David Yakish; **bottom left** Landscape architect: Alana Markle; **bottom right** McGovern garden **30 both** Design: Horiuchi and Solien Landscape **32 top** Design: Bruce Davies, Davies Associates Landscape Architects; **bottom** Design: Horiuchi and Solien Landscape **34 bottom** Longwood Gardens **35 bottom** Design: Fiona Laumenson **38** Design: Kenneth S. Burton, Jr. **45 top** Design: John Scofield **53 bottom** Design: Françoise Kirkman **56** Design: Kenneth S. Burton, Jr. **60** Design: Eichengree Design **61** Design: Scott Kesterson **62 bottom** Landscape design: Chris Fremuth, Dryad Design Company **66** Design: Bob Cowden **67 top** Stone Canyon Gardens; **bottom** Design: Phillip Robinson **74** Design: Kenneth S. Burton, Jr. **79** Landscape design: Lee Haines **84** Design: Elaine Schreve **88 top** Design: Jeffrey B. Glander & Associates; **bottom** Design: David Snow, English Arbor Company **96** Design: Freeland Turner **97 top** Design: Peter Whiteley **102** Design: Leonora R. Burnet and Douglas King Burnet **108** Design: Elaine and Dave Whitehead **121** Michael Shoup garden **122 bottom** Orene Horton garden **126 left** Ray Reddell garden

For additional copies of *Trellises and Arbors* or any other Sunset book, call 1-800-526-5111 or visit us at www.sunset.com.

contents

SUNSET BOOKS

VICE PRESIDENT, GENERAL MANAGER
Richard A. Smeby

VICE PRESIDENT, EDITORIAL DIRECTOR
Bob Doyle

PRODUCTION DIRECTOR
Lory Day

DIRECTOR OF OPERATIONS
Rosann Sutherland

RETAIL SALES DEVELOPMENT MANAGER
Linda Barker

EXECUTIVE EDITOR
Bridget Biscotti Bradley

ART DIRECTOR
Vasken Guiragossian

SPECIAL SALES
Brad Moses

STAFF FOR THIS BOOK

SENIOR EDITOR
Linda J. Selden

MANAGING EDITOR
Esther Ferington

COPY EDITOR/INDEXER
Phyllis Elving

PHOTO EDITOR/STYLIST
Jane Martin

PRINCIPAL PHOTOGRAPHER
Roger Foley

ILLUSTRATOR
Greg Maxson

PROJECT CONSTRUCTION
Jeff Palumbo
Jim Palumbo

PAGE PRODUCTION
Linda M. Bouchard

PRODUCTION COORDINATOR
Eligio Hernandez

PROOFREADER
Mary Roybal

structures for any garden

TRELLISES AND ARBORS LITERALLY LIFT UP YOUR GARDEN, adding a third dimension that can be beautiful, playful, or intriguing, according to your tastes. ■ Trellises, usually simpler and quicker to build, can enliven walls and fences—or stand alone to create a focal point in your garden scheme. Arbors, their more complex cousins, always include an overhead portion; they range from classic arches like the one at left to full-scale grape arbors and pergolas. ■ Most trellises and arbors support climbing plants, which turn them into living ornaments that vary with the seasons. But many gardeners use these same structures without plants. The only real criterion is what looks right in your garden. For some ideas, consider the array of options presented in the pages that follow.

freestanding trellises

Set a trellis on its own in your garden for a visual exclamation point. It's up to you whether the emphasis is on plants brought skyward or on the trellis itself. Even hardworking vegetable trellises can offer good looks (see pages 10–11).

◄ SIMPLICITY ITSELF
Lengths of bamboo lend unobtrusive support to pink Mandevilla blooms in a waterside garden.

▼ ROYAL SPLENDOR
Seated in gravel, a simple wood frame bears a lush burden of Clematis 'Royal Velours'.

▲ PUNCTUATING A HEDGE
A graceful metal obelisk contrasts effectively with the shrubs and hedge growing behind it.

A PLAYFUL BARRIER
Hop vines adorn a
delightful bedstead-
turned-trellis, marking
a garden edge with
unique flair.

VIOLET AND WHITE
The white paint of this pointed obelisk is the perfect counterpoint to the rich purple of Clematis *'Etoile Violette'*.

◀ **CLIMBING TOWER**
A metal tower in a sea of green provides
footholds for a clematis vine.

▼ **PIPING UP**
A gleaming copper trellis soars up from
a container planting. Leaves and flowers
contrast well with its clean, spare lines.

◀ **UPWARD MOBILITY**
Almost hidden amid lush growth, a graceful
metal trellis raises a swirl of blossoms to
eye level and higher.

◀ COUNTRY-GARDEN TRELLIS
Scarlet runner beans climb a
sturdy rustic trellis secured at each
end with a triangle of saplings.

▼ STURDY A-FRAME
An A-frame trellis stands ready
for its crop of vegetables. This self-
supporting trellis style facilitates
vertical gardening in vegetable
plots of any size.

▲ COOK'S FEAST
A long, simple
A-frame for beans
forms a border
in a vegetable and
flower garden.

**◄ TOMATOES
ON DISPLAY**
Cherry tomatoes
flourish in this cage-
style support.

◄ KITCHEN-GARDEN TRELLISES
A mixture of freestanding and wall trellises
makes the most of a cook's garden space.
The woven willow arches in the background
support sugar snap peas.

11

trellises and walls

Traditional trellises dress up house and garden walls and fences, while freestanding trellises may serve as screens, panels, or walls themselves. Bring new life and interest to plain walls with structures like the ones shown here.

▲ A FENCE WITH A DIFFERENCE
Classic white grids add interest to a conventional backyard fence.

▶ TELLING DETAIL
A pocket-size trellis ornaments a wall nook on a New England home.

WALL ARCHES
Made from birch twigs, arch-topped patio trellises combine with flowery clematis to lend character to a featureless wall.

▲ FRAMING AND FAN

Angled white elements work magic on two walls. At top, windowlike framing puts a ceramic pot front and center. Above, silvervein creeper adorns a classic fan trellis.

► **CORNERING THE ROSES**

A trellis isn't always limited to just one wall. Here, roses on grids cover both sides of an exterior house corner.

▲ **WINDOW ACCENT**

A cleverly shaped trellis borders an open window, complemented by the window box below.

► **TIP-TOP TRELLIS**

Built atop a wall, a horizontal trellis lends textural interest and ornamentation to a garden divider.

A SHED TRANSFORMED
Large grids filled with flowering clematis and 'Lucetta' roses make a shed an integral part of the garden that surrounds it.

► **WISTERIA WALL**

A wealth of Chinese wisteria pours across a freestanding trellis screen in pleasing contrast to the grid's crisp geometry.

▼ **DRIVEWAY BEGONE**

The drive to the garage is out of sight, out of mind, thanks to a patio-side screen trellis.

▲ **WELL-PLANTED SPACE**
Climbing roses fill in the grid on this
garden wall, smoothly extending the
planting bed below.

▶ **A BURST OF COLOR**
A gracefully aged screen trellis forms an
effective backdrop for Clematis jackmanii, *a*
popular choice for both trellises and arbors.

▲ COMPLEMENT TO AN ARBOR
Screen trellis "walls" help set the scene
on a deck that's also adorned by a
container garden and a separate arbor.

◄ DEFINING THE DECK
A rose-filled trellis screen marks the side
of a deck that boasts a corner container
garden for hummingbirds and butterflies.

▲ FRAMING A POND
Trellis walls with wide-open framing define
a garden space around a pond without
blocking the view from the other side.

▶ A GRAND TRELLIS

Screen-style trellises don't get much
grander than this pair, joined together
by a densely planted arch arbor.

▼ COURTYARD WALL

A long trellis screen forms the backdrop
to a fine courtyard, adding more plant life
while masking the view beyond.

arbor accents

Arbors don't have to be full-scale "outdoor rooms" to have a pleasing visual effect. Build one in any of the styles shown in these pages to enliven a gate, a path, or a wall, or simply to add distinction to a garden nook.

▲ WELCOME
A white arbor arch offers climbing holds aplenty for vines while marking the entrance to a garden filled with flowers.

◀ WHITE OR PINK?
A refreshing twist on the entry arch offers the visitor not one but two colors of roses, hinting at the variety of colors and plants in the space beyond.

▶ SIMPLY MAGNIFICENT
Wisteria adorns an exquisite yet ultra-simple pathway arbor, made from just a few well-chosen rustic beams.

▶ PAINT IT RED
Classic white is hardly the only choice
for an arbor. A red arch perfectly
complements green and yellow growth.

▼ METAL ELEGANCE
The slender lines of a metal arbor lend
graceful support to garden flowers.

GRACE AND ROSES
Bedecked with roses, this wide white arbor with angled beams and braces divides one garden into two distinct areas.

◄ PATHWAY ARBOR
Complete with crisp lattice walls, a formal white arch flanks a winding path. Climbing roses fill the space overhead.

▲ GARDEN SPACES

A wavy roof and doubled walls add style to an arbor that separates two garden zones linked by a gravel path.

◄ ALASKA DREAMING

On a playful garden structure, striking orcas ride high above a bare supporting frame.

23

▶ **FRAMING A VIEW**
A spectacular teardrop gateway offers support to climbing plants while framing the house and garden beyond. Angled bars on the gates emphasize the structure's unique shape.

▲ **MAKING AN ENTRANCE**
A roofed arbor entrance is the visual high point of an ornate, rose-filled fence.

▶ **BRIDGING THE DISTANCE**
A long, rose-covered arbor top joins house and outbuilding over a broad gateway. At the sides, more climbing roses adorn simple grid walls.

BEYOND THE ORDINARY
Simple trellis and arbor elements, including vertical bars and a triangular "roof," make a fence opening something special.

◄ MOON GATE
Completely covered in rich growth, a curving arbor mirrors the crescent shape of the gate below.

▼ PURPLE WONDERLAND
Painted gates pick up the color of the wisteria blossoms draped on a long arbor overhead.

◄ COME INSIDE
With stunning casual elegance, a flat-topped entry arbor frames a flagstone path leading to the front door.

destination arbors

Certain arbors are meant not as simple accents, but as destinations in themselves. Often located away from the house, these pergolas, walkways, bowers, and other such large structures may offer a bench, chairs, or even a table from which to enjoy the great outdoors.

▼ **AUTUMN ARBOR**

A classic wooden bench provides a fine perspective on the fall colors around a garden grape arbor.

▶ **AN INVITING RETREAT**

Centered beyond an arched arbor, a bench and cushion supply a refuge from care for the garden visitor.

▲ A GRAND PERGOLA

Tree-size posts support a hefty pergola above
a patio furnished with table and chairs.

◀ ROSES ALL THE WAY

Facing arbor benches offer matched views of
'William Baffin' roses to each side and overhead.

▲ SIT BY ME

A cozy arch defines a comfortable conversation
space within the garden.

◀ HIGH RISE

A towering fountain of green frames a cushioned
bench in an otherwise low, flat garden.

▲ WHITE WORKS

White blossoms, white-painted framing, and a light-colored floor make this arbor stand out from a smooth green expanse of lawn. The tree branches overhead provide a natural echo of the arbor roof.

▶ AIRY REFUGE

An open, airy arbor offers just a bit of shade for a garden bench without blocking welcome breezes coming off the water.

▶ LET IN THE LIGHT

Plenty of light and air are available within this inviting arbor. Rounded framing with few crosspieces creates the open effect, and seating options invite visitors to stay.

▼ DINING ALFRESCO

Stained framing and charming rafter ends give a sense of style to a fine pergola built for outdoor dining. Both posts and rafters offer space for climbing vines.

◀ ARBOR COLONNADE
Thickly planted overhead, a walkway arbor supported by stout columns flanks a sunken garden.

▶ PETAL PERFECTION
Fallen rose petals and glowing blooms are a perfect match for a pair of large white arbors and white garden furniture.

▶ WHITE AND GREEN
The vital green of plants, in the garden and climbing the posts, forms a striking contrast with the classic white of this large arbor.

ARBOR WITH A TWIST
Weathered steel bands resting on crushed rock create a unique and surprisingly appealing arbor along which plants have already begun to climb.

A FINE GREEN SETTING
All but hidden by climbing roses, a pergola provides vital but unobtrusive support. A "floor" of grass ties the structure to its surroundings.

▲ LEMON ARBOR
Lemon trees trained across an arbor lend it fragrance, color, and delight.

▶ WISTERIA WALKWAY
Delicate wisteria blossoms fill a sturdy arbor. The bench on the left side of the pathway is a perfect spot to sit and admire the view.

▼ **SNOWY DAY**

Fallen snow emphasizes the geometry of this rustic Maine arbor, on which kiwi vines flourish in summer.

35

trellis projects

NOW THAT YOU HAVE SOME IDEA OF THE DESIGN POSSIBILITIES that a trellis or arbor can add to your landscape, keep reading to see how to turn your vision into reality. Consult this chapter for trellis ideas; for arbor projects, see pages 72–117. The photographs and plans in this chapter offer both inspiration and practical advice for building and installing trellises, from simple fans you can quickly assemble and screw to a post or wall to more elaborate grid and frame combinations that may keep you busy for a day or more.

■ These projects have been carefully selected to present both a broad spectrum of designs and a wide variety of techniques. Feel free to mix and match as you see fit. Build the projects as shown, or change their size, materials, or overall layout to fit your plans and budget. The trellises presented here can be made with basic construction techniques and—with the exception of the rustic pieces—materials you can find in any well-stocked home center. Special features throughout this chapter and the next one offer advice on selecting materials, tools, and hardware and also on construction techniques.

hinged wall trellis

There is nothing like a trellis for dressing up an expanse of blank wall. Whether it is part of your house, a garage, or a garden shed or even stands by itself, any open wall can provide a backdrop for a lovely array of climbing plants. Of course, you'll have the best luck with south-facing walls, but with the right choice of plants, even a wall with a northern exposure can be pressed into service.

This trellis incorporates several innovations that make it a lot nicer than a typical manufactured trellis. First, the grid is made from vinyl lattice. This plastic product is considerably easier to use than wooden lattice. It won't split, it has no splinters, and it never needs painting, so your trellis will look good for years. Second, the trellis is mounted to the wall with a pair of hinges, so you can easily fold it down to paint or wash the wall behind. The hinges also hold the trellis away from the wall, allowing air to circulate behind it. This is better for your plants as well as for your house.

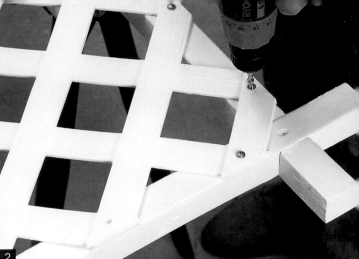

1 Build the Frame

Start by cutting the 8-foot 2 by 2 to the specified lengths. To assemble the frames, cut lap joints at the corners of the 6-foot 2 by 2s and the 39-inch pieces you have cut. To make the lap joints, cut notches halfway through the frame members, 3 inches from the ends; the notch width should match the width of the joining pieces. Make the notches by making repeated cuts with your circular saw and clearing any remaining waste with a chisel, then fit the pieces together. When you are satisfied with the fit of the joints, apply glue to the mating surfaces and assemble the frame. Drive a 1¼-inch screw through each joint to serve as a clamp and as reinforcement. When the glue is dry, prime and paint the frame. While you're at it, prime and paint the two 6-inch blocks as well.

2 Add the Lattice

Cut the lattice to size with your circular saw. The plastic will cut easily with a regular wood-cutting blade, but be sure to support the panel adequately, as it is quite flexible. Flop the cut panel down on the back of the frame. Drill over-

size (¼-inch) holes through the plastic for the 1-inch screws that will fasten it to the frame; the holes need to be oversize to give the plastic room to expand and contract with changes in temperature. Screw the lattice to the back of the frame, but leave the screws slightly loose—again, this allows for expansion and contraction.

3 Install the Hinges

Attach the broad leaves of the hinges to the 6-inch blocks and the long leaves to the back of the trellis frame at the bottom, using 1-inch screws. Screw the blocks to the wall where you want your trellis to be. The blocks should be level with each other. Caulk along the top edges to keep water from wicking behind the blocks. Raise the trellis up against the wall. Attach the hook-and-eye catches

securely to the top of the trellis and to the wall. When it comes time to wash or paint the wall, gently fold the trellis down, plants and all, for access to the wall behind it. When you are finished, simply raise the trellis back into place. To protect your plants, move the trellis only when necessary, and no farther than your work requires.

SHOPPING LIST

- One 8' 2 × 2 for:
  Two 39" frame pieces
  Two 6" hinge blocks
- Two 6' 2 × 2s
- 4' × 8' vinyl lattice, cut to 33" × 66"
- Forty-eight #6 × 1" round-head, stainless-steel screws with washers
- Two 2" rust-resistant strap hinges with screws
- Two rust-resistant hook-and-eye catches
- Weatherproof glue
- Four #6 × 1¼" rust-resistant screws
- Exterior primer and paint
- White exterior caulk

garden grid

Rather than build a fence, why not use a trellis to partition your garden? As a single section, this fencelike unit provides a great boundary for the garden beyond. If you build the grids in multiples, you can use them to enclose a play area or simply to define the boundaries of your property.

MATERIALS

- The basics for this project include treated 6 × 6 posts, preturned finials and moldings for the post tops, 2 × 2s, and 1 × 2s.
- If you have access to a table saw, you can rip 2 × 4s in half for the frame pieces, a process that may yield straighter pieces than precut 2 × 2s.

HOW-TO

- Sink the posts into the ground so they stand about 50 inches above the ground; you can vary the spacing between them, but don't go beyond eight feet or your grid will sag. Dress up the post tops with finials and moldings.
- Backfill one of the posts (see page 78). Leave the second one loose until you finish the grid to make sure the grid fits just right between the posts.
- Make the grid frame from 2 by 2s, joining the corners with lap joints and screws. Then make the grid from 1 by 2s, with lap joints where the pieces intersect (see page 71). Screw the grid frame to the posts, then prime and paint.

fan trellis

As trellis styles go, the fan trellis is one of the most recognizable. What's more, it makes a lot of sense from a design standpoint. Like a plant, a fan trellis starts out narrow at the bottom and then expands as it rises. It's no wonder fan trellises have been popular for so many years. While you can buy fan trellises ready-made, they are really quite simple to put together yourself. That way you can vary the size to suit your purpose.

MATERIALS

- Start with six 1 × 1 strips of wood. Look for the clearest pieces you can find (those with the fewest knots).
- Use 1 × 2 strips for the crosspieces.

HOW-TO

- Clamp the strips together near the bottom, drill two holes through them 4 to 5 inches apart, and bolt the pieces together with carriage bolts (see diagram).
- Spread the fan outward, nailing straight crosspieces in place as you go; you may find that an extra set of hands is a big help with this operation.
- Paint or stain the trellis as you see fit, then screw it in place to a wall or, for a freestanding version, a stake. For a wall mount, use scraps of rot-resistant lumber to space the trellis away from the wall.

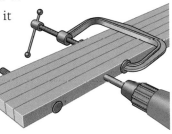

simple trellis

Traditional trellis designs like this one often call for the crisp milled shapes of what is loosely called "lath"—lumber that typically ranges from about ¼ to ½ inch thick and ¾ to 2 inches wide.

MATERIALS

- Rot-resistant woods such as cedar and redwood are good lath choices, as is pressure-treated lumber, if you can find the right dimensions. Untreated pine and other woods will also work if painted or stained.

HOW-TO

- Connect the pieces with short screws; predrill the holes to avoid splitting the wood.
- Mount the trellis by screwing it to the wall. You can also mount a simple trellis with hinges (see page 39). This allows easy access to the wall for maintenance.

stylish vegetable trellis

Many vegetable plants benefit from the support and elevation of a trellis. Peas, runner beans, and even some cucumbers and squashes will climb. Vertical vegetable gardening also helps keep your garden compact, and it brings the results of your labors to a convenient height for harvest.

While gardeners often put together vegetable trellises from a few scraps, it is worth a little extra time and effort to build one that enhances the look of your garden as well as its productivity. The attractive example shown below is especially simple to construct. For additional vegetable trellis projects, see pages 44–45.

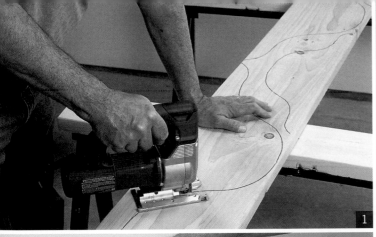
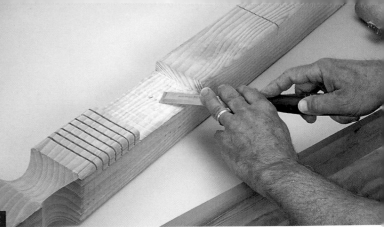

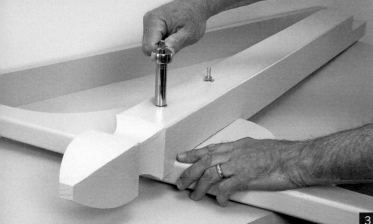
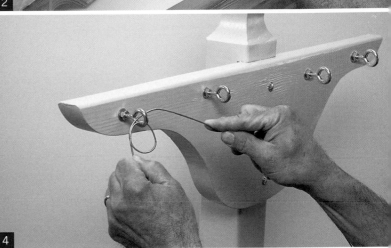

1 Cut the Crosspieces

Sketch shapes for an upper and a lower crosspiece on a piece of cardboard; the exact curves aren't important. Trace two of each on the 2 by 10, fitting the two longer pieces end to end and nestling the other two in the remaining areas. Set the board on sawhorses and cut the pieces with a jigsaw.

2 Notch the Posts

Notch the posts to hold the crosspieces. Mark for the top of the upper crosspiece about 1 inch below the finial cut, and for the top of the lower crosspiece 8 inches below the bottom of the upper one. With your circular saw set to a ¾-inch depth, make several cuts through each marked notch area. Then finish the notch with a chisel.

3 Attach the Crosspieces

Prime and paint the posts and the crosspieces. Seat the crosspieces in the notches. Drill two ¼-inch holes through each crosspiece and as far as possible into the post; set the crosspiece aside to extend the holes all the way through the post. Attach the crosspieces to the posts with carriage bolts.

4 String the Guide Wires

Drill ¼-inch holes for the eyebolts near both ends of each upper crosspiece and also about 6 inches out from the posts. Thread nuts and washers on the eyebolts, push the eyebolts through the holes, and lock them in place with more washers and nuts. Add eyebolts to the lower crosspieces as well. Dig postholes about 3 feet deep and set the posts in place, tamping down the soil. String wire between the crosspieces, feeding it through an eyebolt twice and twisting it with pliers, then running it to the corresponding eye on the opposite post (it doesn't have to be taut) and securing it the same way.

SHOPPING LIST

- One 8' 2 × 10 for:
  Two upper crosspieces
  (each 9¼" × 36")
  Two lower crosspieces
  (each 6" × 24")
- Two 7' 4 × 4 rot-resistant
  fence posts with finials
- Eight ¼-20 × 5" galvanized carriage bolts with washers and nuts
- Sixteen ¼ × 4" rust-resistant eyebolts with 32 washers and 32 nuts
- Exterior primer and paint
- 14-gauge galvanized wire

low vegetable trellis

There are any number of vegetable plants that don't need a tall trellis but still benefit from a little organization. Enter the low vegetable trellis. Like a good office manager, this humble bit of outdoor woodwork provides support for plants that need it without getting in the way of production.

MATERIALS

- The main pieces are made from 2 × 2s; the dividers are ¾-inch dowels.
- Pressure-treated wood will last longer, but you'll be able to get several seasons out of regular lumber if you prefer to keep your vegetables away from the rot-resisting chemicals of treated lumber.

HOW-TO

- Construction is simple. Cut the horizontal frame pieces to length, depending on the size of your garden, and then drill matching holes in them for the connecting dowels.
- Cut the legs to 16 inches—12 inches to stand above the ground and 4 inches to go into the ground for stability. Attach the legs to the horizontal pieces. For added stability, you can cut lap joints where the legs join the horizontals.
- If horizontal pieces sag, add a leg in the middle.
- Slide the dowels into place, using a dab of weatherproof glue in each hole. After the glue dries, saw off the dowel ends flush with the frame.

vegetable panel

If you are like many vegetable gardeners, you probably rotate your crops to avoid disease and to rest the soil. Here's a lightweight trellis you can move easily as the need arises.

MATERIALS

- The wooden trellis parts are made from 1 × 2s. Nylon cords form the verticals for plants to climb.

- In the trellis at left, a copper fish adds a sense of whimsy. Consider your own personal touch to make this panel please the eye as well as the taste buds.

HOW-TO

- Screw the horizontal pieces to the outside verticals, alternating them from one face to the other. Leave about 12 inches of the verticals to sink into the ground.
- Cut angles on the ends of the diagonal pieces to fit against the verticals. Weave the diagonal pieces and the center vertical through the horizontal pieces. Screw them to the horizontals to prevent the trellis from racking, and screw the diagonals to the center vertical at the top.
- Tie the nylon cords in place.

garden cages

Wood isn't the only good trellis material. Here, plastic pipe teams up with vinyl-covered mesh to form portable vegetable cages.

MATERIALS

- The support structure of these cages is made from lengths of rigid plastic pipe. Pipe fittings make the connections between the pipes.
- The trellis "walls" are vinyl-covered wire mesh. Look for mesh with at least 2- by 4-inch openings so you'll be able to reach in to harvest your vegetables.

HOW-TO

- Cut the pipe pieces to the desired lengths. Plastic pipe cuts easily with a hack saw.
- Use the appropriate cement to glue the pipes to the fittings.
- Cut the wire mesh to size with wire cutters. Using pliers, bend the ends around the pipe frame. Wire ties will help hold the mesh in place.

MATERIALS AND TOOLS

Most trellises and arbors can be built using basic carpenter's tools and standard lumber. Consult these two pages to make the best choices for your project.

Lumber Options

Lumber is where most arbor and trellis projects begin. And because wood takes the biggest bite out of your project budget, it pays to learn the basics of lumber types and terms before you begin shopping.

WHAT TYPE IS BEST? For starters, lumber is divided into softwoods (from evergreens) and hardwoods (from deciduous trees). Of the two types, softwoods are much less expensive and more readily available. All of the projects in this book are built from softwoods.

Woods from different trees have specific properties. For example, redwood and cedar heartwoods—the darker, denser part of the wood, from the tree's core—are naturally resistant to decay. This makes them ideal for arbors and trellises—but because they're costly, many people use less expensive spruce, pine, or fir and protect them from rot by painting or staining them.

Using pressure-treated lumber is another option. Lumber treated with CCA (chromated copper arsenate), once the most popular choice, is being phased out and replaced with wood that has been treated with other preservatives. CCA-treated wood has a distinctive green color; newer types of pressure-treated lumber have their own look, often brownish gray. If you use pressure-treated lumber, wear gloves, goggles, and a dust mask, and never burn leftover pieces. Wash up carefully after working, and contain any sawdust as much as possible.

If you intend for your project to be in direct contact with the ground, be sure to purchase lumber that is rated for ground contact. Wood with a lesser rating won't last long if it is left in contact with soil.

LUMBER SIZES Keep in mind that the nominal size of most softwood—that is, its name— is bigger than the actual size. That's because the wood is measured before being dried and surfaced. A standard 2 by 4 is actually about $1\frac{1}{2}$ by $3\frac{1}{2}$ inches. Likewise, a 4 by 4 is actually about $3\frac{1}{2}$ by $3\frac{1}{2}$ inches.

LUMBER GRADES Structural lumber and timbers are rated for strength. The most common grades you'll come across at a typical home center are No. 1 and No. 2. For most outdoor projects, the difference is purely cosmetic—

trellis atop a raised bed

Standing as a sentinel at the edge of a patio or flanking the side of a path, this raised bed/trellis combination adds a sense of substance to an otherwise flat landscape. Cover it with flowering vines to help the structure recede, giving way to a softer, more natural effect.

Construction is straightforward—the raised bed is simply a box assembled from 2 by 6s, covered with a log facade. The trellis is a cage of fairly slender slats screwed together. A secondary "wall" of slats runs through the center to provide additional support for your plants.

No. 1 wood has fewer knots and will generally look better than No. 2 wood.

Premium woods such as redwood and cedar often have their own grades. Redwood, for example, is usually graded for its appearance and its percentage of heartwood.

One of the best ways to save money on a project is to identify and use the most appropriate grade—not the costliest—for each element; you'll find that you don't need to use the highest grade of lumber for the entire structure.

Tool Choices

Building great trellises and arbors doesn't have to involve an extensive tool kit. You can build any of the projects in this book with a selection of basic carpentry and home maintenance tools. The tools shown here are among those you'll need.

HANDSAW—FOR THE FEW CUTS YOU CAN'T MAKE WITH A POWER SAW

DUST MASK

CHISELS—FOR TRIMMING AND CLEANING UP JOINERY

SAFETY GLASSES—FOR PROTECTING YOUR MOST IMPORTANT TOOLS

ANGLE SQUARE—FOR MEASURING AND LAYING OUT AS WELL AS FOR GUIDING YOUR CIRCULAR SAW

CIRCULAR SAW—FOR MAKING STRAIGHT CUTS IN LUMBER AND PLYWOOD

HEARING PROTECTORS

ROUTER—FOR MAKING DECORATIVE EDGES

FRAMING SQUARE—FOR CHECKING ACCURACY OF ASSEMBLIES AND MAKING LAYOUTS

For specific projects, you may also use a combination square and a level; a hammer, screwdrivers, and wrenches; a utility knife; and clamps. Some tools are necessities, while others simply make certain tasks easier. Add the latter to your toolbox as your skills grow and your bank account allows.

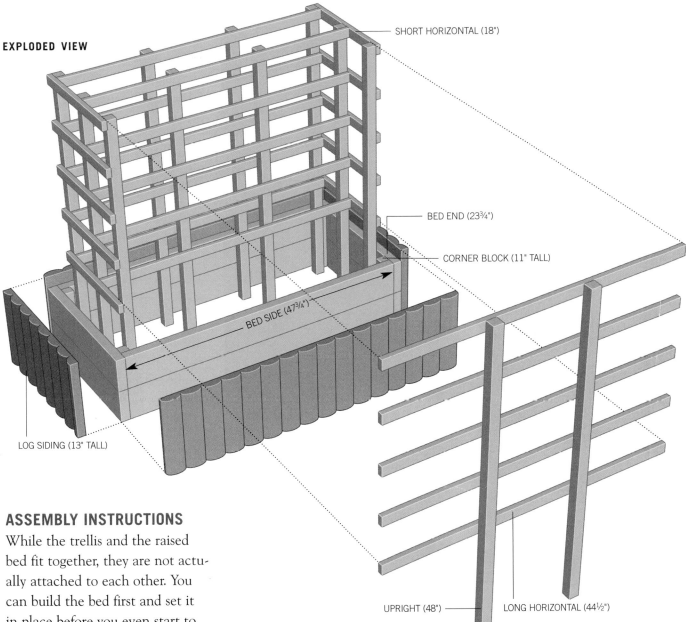

EXPLODED VIEW

SHORT HORIZONTAL (18")

BED END (23¾")

CORNER BLOCK (11" TALL)

BED SIDE (47¾")

LOG SIDING (13" TALL)

UPRIGHT (48")

LONG HORIZONTAL (44½")

ASSEMBLY INSTRUCTIONS

While the trellis and the raised bed fit together, they are not actually attached to each other. You can build the bed first and set it in place before you even start to build the trellis. Use pressure-treated lumber for the bed pieces and the uprights, as these parts will be in direct contact with the soil. You can use almost any kind of wood for the siding and the horizontal pieces, since they will be less prone to rot. After you set the raised bed in place, center the trellis inside it. Fill the bed with your favorite soil mix. If you don't have a favorite mix, start with 3 parts topsoil to 1 part compost.

SHOPPING LIST

- Three 8' 2 × 6s for:
  Four bed side pieces
  Four bed end pieces
- Eleven 4' 2 × 2s for:
  Twelve uprights
  Four corner blocks
- Ten 8' 1 × 2s for:
  Ten short horizontals
  Fifteen long horizontals

- Eight 8' lengths of 3"-wide log siding
- One pound of #10 × 3" rust-resistant screws
- One pound of #8 × 2" rust-resistant screws
- Landscape fabric (about 28" × 55")
- ⅜" rust-resistant staples
- Weatherproof glue
- Semitransparent exterior stain

1 Build the Bed

Cut the bed sides, ends, and corner blocks to length (see diagram, page 49). Place two side pieces with long edges together and use 3-inch screws to attach a corner block across them at each end. Repeat the process to make the second side. Stand one side on edge and attach the two end pieces, using 3-inch screws to attach each to both the corner block and the end of a side piece for added strength. Attach the other end pieces and the second side to complete the box.

2 Attach Landscape Fabric

Drape landscape fabric over the bottom of the completed bed. Fold the edges over and staple the fabric to the bed (doubling the fabric at the edges makes the connection stronger). Trim away any excess. The landscape fabric will help keep the soil in the bed from washing out of the planter.

3 Cut the Siding

Cut the log siding to length. Although you can do this with a circular saw, you'll get more consistent results with a power miter saw (also called a chop saw). Fasten a straight piece of scrap lumber to the saw fence; most saws have screw holes for this purpose, or you can use small C-clamps. Clamp a small block along the scrap wood the right distance from the blade. Cut the siding and attach it around the bed using 3-inch screws.

4 Build the Ends of the Trellis

For each end unit of the trellis, cut the short horizontal pieces to length. Space out three uprights evenly on a flat surface (if you don't have room on a workbench, the floor works). Using 2-inch screws, attach a short horizontal piece to the three uprights, flush with the top ends, adding a dab of weatherproof glue at each joint to keep the trellis from racking. Attach four more horizontals, spacing them 6 inches apart and continuing to dab glue.

5 Connect the Trellis Ends

Cut the long horizontal trellis pieces to length. Prop the end units up and attach the long horizontal pieces between them, screwing the horizontals to the insides of the uprights with 2-inch screws. Start by installing all the horizontals on one side, and add two uprights. Then add the horizontals and uprights that go in the middle, and finally attach the pieces to form the other long side. Again, use a dab of glue at each joint for increased strength. Finish the entire assembly with semi-transparent wood stain.

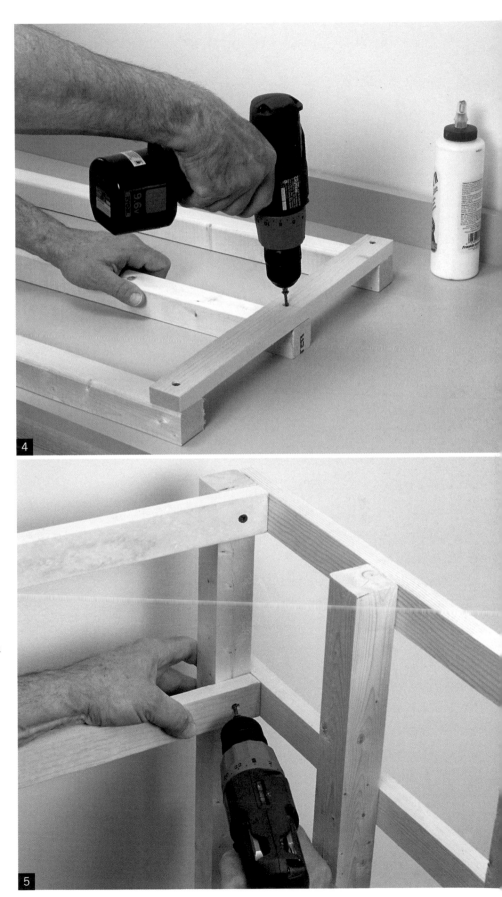

rustic trellis

As a support for climbing plants or simply as a vertical element for your wildflower garden, this rustic trellis is quick to build and a great way to use up debris from your spring pruning. As you trim your trees, be on the lookout for interestingly shaped branches to contrast with the straight ones in the trellis.

MATERIALS

- This trellis is made from a variety of straight and curved branches.
- Try to accumulate about 50 to 100 percent more material than you think you'll need. As you gather the pieces, sort them into piles according to diameter.
- To bend new curves, use fresh-cut branches; older wood may be too brittle.

HOW-TO

- As you assemble the pieces, use larger-diameter pieces for the main framework elements, smaller-diameter pieces for the lesser elements.
- Fasten the pieces together with rust-resistant nails or screws. Predrill the holes to avoid splitting the wood.
- Keep the trellis in place and slightly off the ground by wiring it to 36-inch lengths of ½-inch pipe driven into the ground.

simple bamboo trellis

Bamboo is another material that makes great-looking trellises. You can use it to make simple grids like the one at right or to build structures that are much more elaborate.

MATERIALS

- Bamboo is available in diameters ranging from approximately 1/2 to 4 inches and in lengths up to 12 feet.
- Secure joints between pieces with 15-gauge galvanized steel or copper wire.

HOW-TO

- Develop a hierarchy of sizes for the different elements of your trellis. Use large-diameter pieces for main supports and smaller diameters for the other pieces.
- To make connections, drill through the bamboo pieces where they intersect. Feed a length of wire through the holes (see diagram), then wrap the ends around the bamboo. Finish the connection by twisting the ends of the wire together.

- To conceal the wire, wrap the joints with black hemp twine.
- Bamboo will rot quickly if left in contact with soil. To make it last longer, slip the pieces over 36-inch lengths of 1/2-inch rebar driven into the ground. The solid internodes inside the bamboo will keep the trellis from sliding down the pipe. If you don't mind seeing the pipes, use longer pieces and simply wire the trellis to them.

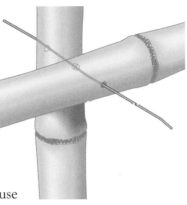

twig grid

This variation on the rustic trellis uses only straight lengths of wood—here, trimmings from fruit trees. Despite these humble beginnings, the end result is quite pleasing. The finished structure is about 3 feet wide and just over 7 feet tall.

MATERIALS

- To duplicate the trellis shown, you'll need two uprights about 1 1/2 inches in diameter and ten additional pieces about 1 inch in diameter.
- If you lack a source for tree trimmings, you could substitute bamboo or 1 × 1 stakes from the lumberyard.

HOW-TO

- Cut pieces to size with a pruning saw. Trim away any side branches.
- Fasten pieces together with rust-resistant screws, predrilling holes to avoid splitting the wood.
- Reinforce the joints by wrapping them with 15-gauge galvanized steel wire.
- To anchor the trellis, drive two 36-inch lengths of 1/2-inch rebar into the ground, leaving about 10 inches exposed. Wire the trellis legs to the rebar.

bifold trellis

The two panel grids shown below join at a slight angle, giving this lovely bifold trellis its name. While the panels do not actually pivot, the angle serves a couple of purposes. It gives the trellis a more three-dimensional look than a simple flat trellis has. And because the posts are not set in a straight line, the trellis is somewhat more stable.

MATERIALS

■ If you plan to paint your trellis, you can use standard, construction-grade lumber for all the aboveground pieces. If you prefer to stain the trellis or let it weather naturally, choose pressure-treated wood or a type that is naturally rot-resistant, such as cedar or redwood.

■ Make the grid pieces from 2 × 2s and the uprights from 2 × 6s. Use a 2 × 4 where the two panels meet.

HOW-TO

■ Each grid is flanked by 2 by 6s to which pairs of 2 by 2s are screwed, forming tracks to hold the grid in place. Install one 2 by 2 on each upright. Sink short pressure-treated posts into the ground as anchors, and screw the uprights to them.

■ Arrange the 2 by 2s as a grid and screw them together at the intersection points. Raise each grid into place, then attach the second 2 by 2 to each upright to secure the grids.

■ Use a 2 by 4 as trim to cover the opening between the two uprights where the panels meet.

Nails, screws, and bolts are essential for outdoor projects—without them, it would be difficult to put boards or beams together!

Nails

Hot-dipped galvanized, aluminum, or stainless-steel nails are best for outdoor construction, because they resist rust. Common nails have a head and a thick shank and are good for holding structural pieces together. Finish nails are more easily hidden beneath the surface of the wood.

Standard nail sizes are given in "pennies," with the word "penny" abbreviated as "d" (from the Latin *denarius*, a type of Roman coin). The higher the number, the longer the nail. Choose nails about twice as long as the thickness of the top piece you'll be nailing through (slightly less if you are nailing two pieces of the same thickness). Most 2-by lumber is secured with 8d and 16d nails.

Screws

Coated or galvanized deck screws offer several advantages over nails. They don't pop out as readily, and their coating is less likely to be damaged during installation. Since they aren't pounded in, you don't have to worry about hammer dents. They're also easier than nails to remove when repairs are required.

Screws are surprisingly easy to drive into softwoods if you use an electric drill or screw gun with an adjustable clutch and a screwdriver tip. While you can often drive a screw straight into the wood, it is better to predrill the holes to avoid splitting the wood. Choose screws that are long enough to penetrate about twice the top member's thickness (for example, use 2½-inch screws to join two 2 by 4s or 2 by 6s).

Deck screws are quite good for assembling most outdoor projects, but they are not typically used in structural (load-bearing) applications. It's best to use nails, lag screws, or bolts to fasten rafters or posts to beams. The lag screw is a cross between a screw and a bolt. Lag screws are considerably larger in diameter than typical deck screws and have hexagonal heads. Lag screws must be tightened with a wrench or a ratchet and socket.

Bolts

For heavy-duty fastening, choose bolts. Most are galvanized steel, but aluminum, stainless-steel, and brass bolts are also available. Bolts go into predrilled holes and are secured by nuts (always put a washer under the nut for a secure connection). The machine bolt has a hexagonal head and is used with a nut and two washers; it must be tightened with a wrench at each end. The carriage bolt has a rounded self-anchoring head that digs into the wood as the nut is tightened.

Bolts are classified by diameter (¼- to ½-inch bolts are typically used for outdoor projects) and length (½ inch and up). To give the nut a firm bite, select a bolt that is ½ to 1 inch longer than the combined thickness of the pieces to be joined.

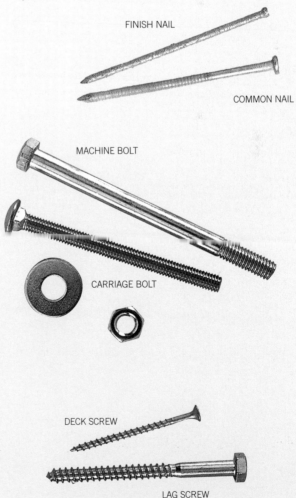

FINISH NAIL

COMMON NAIL

MACHINE BOLT

CARRIAGE BOLT

DECK SCREW

LAG SCREW

container trellis

D on't let the lack of a suitable wall or a large garden keep you from the joys of growing a climbing plant. All you really need is some wire mesh to serve as a trellis and a container in which to root the plant, and you're in business. With a little more effort, you can build a custom planter/ trellis like the one below. It uses a hidden plastic flowerpot (to help keep rot at bay), some galvanized wire, and some lumber to create an elegant accent for your patio or deck. If you choose to add casters to the underside, it can become a mobile garden that you can move about with the seasons.

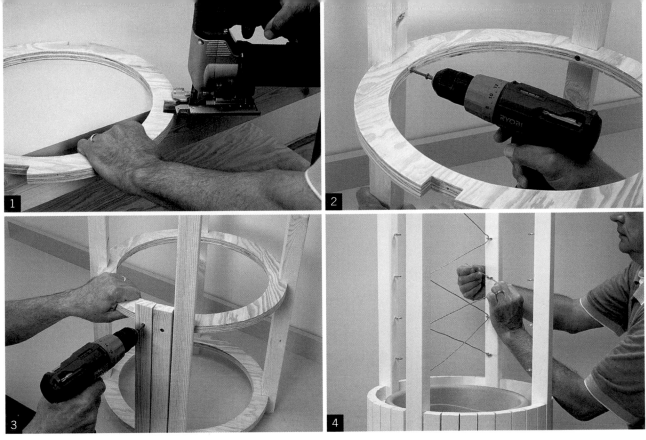

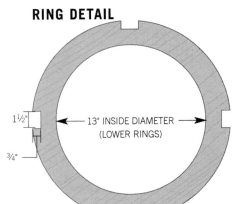

RING DETAIL

1½"
13" INSIDE DIAMETER
(LOWER RINGS)
¾"

1 Cut the Rings

For the rings, cut the three circles 17³/₁₆ inches in diameter. Drill an access hole inside each piece to make the interior cutouts. Cut the inside diameter of the two lower rings to 13 inches, and cut the inside diameter of the top ring to 14³/₁₆ inches. Then cut four notches in each ring (see diagram above).

2 Attach to the Uprights

Glue and screw the rings to the uprights, positioning the top of the middle ring 14½ inches from the bottom and the other rings 1½ inches in from the ends. To avoid splitting the wood, predrill ⁷/₆₄-inch pilot holes through the rings and into the uprights.

3 Attach the Slats

Cut the 1 by 2 slats to the length specified below. (If you have a power miter saw, you can clamp a stop on an extension fence to avoid measuring each piece—see page 50.) Space the slats around the bottom two rings and screw them in place, first drilling and counterboring the screw holes to avoid splitting the wood.

4 Weave the Guide Wires

Fill the screw holes with wood filler, then prime and paint the planter. Put the flowerpot in place, with its lip overlapping the middle ring, before proceeding. Install the screw eyes on the insides of the uprights 4 inches apart, starting about 4 inches above the middle ring. Weave the wire back and forth between the screw eyes.

SHOPPING LIST

- Three 24" × 24" pieces of ¾" AC exterior plywood for rings
- Four 4' 2 × 2s for uprights
- Six 8' 1 × 2s for thirty-two 15¹⁵/₁₆" slats
- Sixty-eight #8 × 1⅝" rust-resistant screws
- Twenty-eight ³/₁₆"-diameter × ¾" rust-resistant screw eyes
- Weatherproof glue
- Wood filler, exterior primer, and exterior paint
- 14"-diameter plastic flowerpot with outside lip
- 18-gauge galvanized wire

A-frame trellis

A combination of features makes this variation on the classic A-frame trellis a versatile addition to almost any garden. The low-slung planter boxes perform much like miniature raised beds, providing an excellent place to root climbing plants. The twin trellises can show off any number of flowering vines, while the entire assembly can serve as a gateway, albeit a low one, to a garden path. That's a lot of garden structure in a relatively compact package.

Before both sides are screwed together and the beds are filled and planted, the side units will be top-heavy. Be sure to have a helper for the final assembly. If the weight of the trellis grids tends to spread the unit apart, you can drive stakes or short lengths of rebar just outside the boxes.

1 Assemble the Beds

Cut the bed sides, ends, and corner blocks to the specified lengths (see "Shopping List"). Place two blocks on your work surface with two bed ends lying next to each other on top of them. Make sure the ends of the pieces are flush. Screw the ends to the blocks with 3-inch screws. Repeat the process to make a second end unit. Screw the bed sides to both the blocks and the end pieces for added strength. Construct a second bed the same way.

2 Make the Grids

Cut the slats for the grids and lay out half of them, putting the vertical pieces down first. Allow about 3½ inches between slats. Make sure the ends of the horizontal slats are aligned at both ends. Drive a 1¼-inch screw through each intersection, adding a dab of weatherproof glue. Make the second grid the same way.

3 Attach the Uprights

For each grid, position an upright against the ends of the horizontal slats. The top of the upright should align with the second slat from the top. Drill ⅛-inch pilot holes through the upright into the ends of the horizontal slats and screw the upright to the slats with 3-inch screws. Attach a second upright to the other end of the slats.

4 Complete the Assembly

Recruit a helper for the final assembly. Stand one trellis vertically over a planter box with its front side about 4 inches from the front of the box. Drill a ¼-inch hole through the upright and the top part of the planter. Install a carriage bolt in the hole; use a hammer to help seat the head. Repeat for the other upright. After each unit is in place, screw the top horizontal slats together to lock in the angle, then drill for and install a second bolt through each upright. Apply semitransparent wood stain.

After you fill the planter boxes with soil, check to make sure the finished unit is not top-heavy. If it is, drive reinforcing stakes just outside each box to keep the sides from spreading.

SHOPPING LIST

- Five 8' 2 × 6s for:
  Eight 47¾" bed sides
  Eight 10" bed ends
- Two 4' 2 × 2s for eight 11" corner blocks
- Thirty-six 8' 1 × 2s for:
  Eighteen 84" vertical slats
  Thirty-six 47¾" horizontal slats
- Four 8' 2 × 2 uprights

- Two pounds of #10 × 3" rust-resistant screws
- Two pounds of #6 × 1¼" rust-resistant screws
- Eight ¼-20 × 3½" galvanized carriage bolts with washers and nuts
- Weatherproof glue
- Semitransparent exterior stain

pipe dreams

A trip through the plumbing aisle at your local home center will yield another batch of trellis makings: copper pipe and fittings. With a tubing cutter, a propane torch, flux, and solder, you can create any number of different trellis designs. The one shown here is a simple tower with a pyramid on top. If you prefer not to solder, you can use epoxy to make the connections.

MATERIALS

- Copper pipe comes in both flexible and rigid forms. For straight pieces, the rigid variety is the best choice, since it is already straight and tends to stay that way. For curved elements, you can readily bend the flexible copper tubing, but getting it to bend to the exact shape you are after takes some practice.
- To make connections, buy copper pipe fittings: elbows for corners, tees for intersections, and couplings where you need to join straight sections.

HOW-TO

- Cut the pieces to the desired lengths with a tubing cutter (available in the plumbing section).
- To remove any oxidation, use fine sandpaper or steel wool to polish the parts of the pipe that will be inside the fittings. Also polish the insides of the fittings.
- Coat the polished areas with flux. Be careful not to get any flux on your clothing—it is an acid and will eat holes in fabric.
- Soldering involves an open flame, so take appropriate precautions. Don't work near dry or flammable materials, or outdoors on a windy day.
- Fit each pair of pipe pieces together and heat them with a propane torch. When the metal is hot enough, touch the solder to the joint and let it flow in.
- Wipe away any excess flux and solder with a damp rag.

climbing the ladder

One way to use copper pipe is for the "rungs" in a ladder-style trellis. The pipe slides through holes drilled in wooden vertical pieces. For a more finished look, you can glue or solder caps onto the pipe ends.

MATERIALS

- For the horizontals, use ½-inch rigid copper tubing.
- The verticals in this example are a mix of 4 × 4s and 2 × 3s, with 2 × 4 top and bottom plates.

HOW-TO

- Drill a series of holes ¾ inch in diameter, their centers spaced about 8 inches apart, through the verticals. Lay out and drill one vertical first, then use it as a template as you drill the other pieces. A drill guide will help keep the holes straight.
- Nail the verticals to the top and bottom plates. Fasten the bottom plate to the ground with pole barn spikes or lengths of rebar driven through holes drilled in the board. Attach the top plate to the underside of the soffit, screwing through into the framing.
- Slide the pipes into position. If necessary, drill pilot holes at an angle through the verticals and into the pipes and drive a few finish nails to hold the pipes in place.

wire on the wall

Espalier, the art of training plants against a flat surface, can work well in both formal and informal gardens. As shown here, the basic idea is to attach a series of wires to a wall in order to create a geometric pattern. Over time, you encourage a plant to follow the lines of the pattern, trimming away any growth that does not conform.

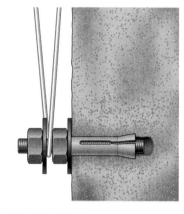

MATERIALS

- To attach to a wooden wall or fence, use screw eyes to anchor the wires. For masonry walls, use expanding anchors (see diagram).
- Use turnbuckles to keep the wires tight, as shown in the photo at right.

HOW-TO

- Start by determining your pattern. For a formal geometric pattern, measure very carefully so the lines remain parallel and the spacing is accurate. Even small errors can be painfully obvious in a pattern that is supposed to be precise. Informal patterns are more forgiving.
- Drill holes and install the screw eyes or anchors.
- Stretch the wire from point to point.
- Start your plants growing along the wires. Prune away growth that does not conform to the pattern. Be patient. It can take years for a pattern to fill in completely.

rustic screen

A trellis doesn't have to be a small endeavor. For large spaces, build a trellis on a scale to match the environment. If you choose a rustic look, you can save considerably over the cost of a similar-size trellis built of lumberyard purchases.

MATERIALS

- For a trellis of this scale, you'll need access to a good supply of saplings or pruning leftovers from large trees.
- If you can get it soon after it is cut, almost any wood can be bent into the gentle curves shown here. For more severe curves, try to find willow pieces.
- The major framing elements in this trellis are 2 to 4 inches in diameter, the filler pieces about 1 inch in diameter.

HOW-TO

- Joining the major pieces is easier if you notch them (see page 82). Use large nails or pole barn spikes to make the connections.
- Nail or screw the smaller pieces in place.
- The uprights can be spiked to the ground (see page 83) or secured to rebar stakes.

garden to go

Don't let the lack of a large open space limit your garden aspirations. Container gardening opens up a whole world of possibilities, particularly when the container is coupled with a built-in trellis. (For a more vertical container trellis, see pages 56–57.)

MATERIALS

- The wood used for this planter is redwood, though cedar would also be a good choice. Use 1 × 6s for the box and 1 × 1 stakes for the trellis.
- Build the base to fit around a plastic planter box (or two) to keep the soil and water away from the wood.
- If you intend to move the planter, install heavy-duty casters for it to roll on.

HOW-TO

- Assemble the box with screws. Add blocks inside the corners, both as reinforcement and as attachment points for casters.

- Screw the trellis uprights directly to the back of the planter box. Screw the horizontals in place only after the verticals are installed. Angled cuts at the ends add a nice touch.

obelisk

An obelisk or garden tower is a great way to add a sense of verticality to your garden. Its crisp geometry will be a focal point long before your plants climb to its top. Once your climbers are established, the contrast between the natural and the constructed elements will only enhance the appeal. The obelisk shown here is made from pressure-treated lumber, left to weather naturally. You can make yours the same way, or paint it a jaunty yellow or jade green to add color to your garden the year around. If you have difficulty finding treated lath, paint is the best way to protect the untreated wood.

ASSEMBLY INSTRUCTIONS

Building the obelisk isn't that difficult, but there are some tricky angled cuts you'll need to make to get the legs to splay correctly. The good thing is that even if you are off a little bit, the tower will still work. Because the legs are so long, you can flex them slightly to get everything to line up.

1 Cut the Tongue

Mark the cut post for a tongue on the end. The tongue will be wider at its base than at its shoulders. It should be 1 inch wide at its base and taper to ½ inch at the shoulders, which should be 3⅜ inches above the post end. Set your circular saw to make a cut 1½ inches deep. Make a cut to establish one of the shoulders, then cut along the tapered line you have marked on that side. Cut from both sides of the post with your circular saw, then use a handsaw to remove the wood in the middle that the circular saw can't reach. Cut the other side of the tongue in the same way.

2 Attach the Legs

The tops of the legs are cut on a compound angle—that is, the circular saw is run across the pieces at an angle with its blade also tilted. The magic number is 6 degrees. Make the cuts 6 degrees off square with the blade also tilted 6 degrees. Position the legs against the post tongue and screw them to the post with 2-inch screws, predrilling the holes to avoid splitting the wood.

3 Install the Spreaders

Cut the spreaders to length, angling the ends, and screw them to the legs with 2-inch screws about 10 inches above the bottom ends. (Again, predrill the holes to avoid splitting the wood.) You may need to flex the legs a little to make the spreaders fit.

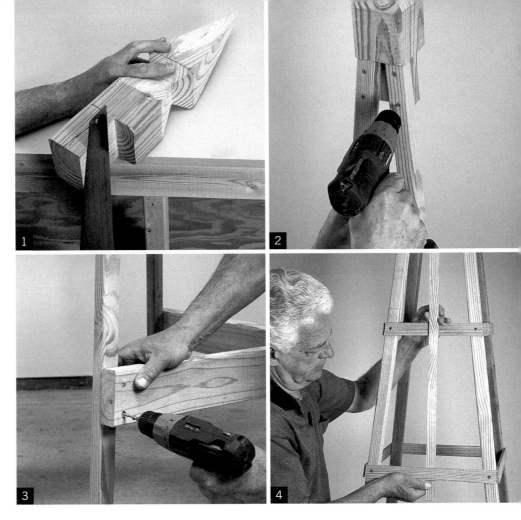

4 Attach the Inner Pieces

Cut the crosspieces, angling the ends, and space them 15 inches apart on the legs, starting from the top of the spreaders. The ¼-inch lath is prone to splitting, so before you drive any screws, predrill ⅛-inch pilot holes. Countersink the holes so the screw heads will sit flush with the surface; countersinking also helps keep the wood from splitting. Screw the crosspieces to the legs with 1¼-inch screws. Weave the verticals over and under the crosspieces. Fasten the verticals to the post and the spreaders with 1¼-inch screws.

SHOPPING LIST

- One 4 × 4 fence post with finial, cut to 17⅜"
- Four 8' 2 × 2s for 93½" legs
- One 8' 2 × 4 for four 22" spreaders
- Four 4' pieces of ¼" × 1½" lath for:
  Four 17⅝" lower crosspieces
  Four 14" middle crosspieces
  Four 10½" upper crosspieces
- Four 7' pieces of ¼" × 1" lath for four verticals
- Eight 5' pieces of ¼" × 1" lath for eight 53" verticals
- One pound of #8 × 2" rust-resistant screws
- One pound of #6 × 1¼" rust-resistant screws

classic rose tower

Quite often, the best solution to a problem is the simplest one. As garden towers go, it doesn't get much simpler than a single 6 by 6 sunk into the ground with pipes attached near the top to support a rose bush. The minimal structure provides what's needed without distracting from the flowering glory it secures.

MATERIALS

- Use a 6 × 6 post about 3 feet longer than the intended final height of your tower.
- Make the arms from 1/2-inch steel pipe.

HOW-TO

- Building this tower is about as straightforward as it gets. Dig a hole about 3 feet deep. Set the post in place and backfill (see page 78).
- To install the pipes, drill holes through the post with a spade bit and drive the pipe through. Add pipe caps to the ends of the arms.

formal garden pyramid

With its slender, geometric form, this graceful wood pyramid makes an excellent focal point for the surrounding flower garden. The structure's straight lines provide a counterpoint to the curving nature of the garden plantings and contrast nicely with rounded flower blossoms. At the top, a small planter loaded with blooms caps the whole affair.

MATERIALS

- To achieve the delicate lines of this pyramid, you'll need thinner sections of wood than are commonly available. Buy 1 × 3s, then have them planed down to ½ inch thick.
- The finished pyramid should be 60 inches high, with a leg spread of about 22 inches.

HOW-TO

- Glue two pieces for each leg to form an L-shaped profile, clamping them in place while they dry.
- Cut long miters at the top of each leg, then glue and nail the mitered ends together using 8d finish nails, predrilling to avoid splitting the wood.
- Screw the crosspieces in place inside the legs, add the center verticals, and prime and paint.

treelike tower

With the right plants and this clever tower, you can create the illusion of a giant flowering shrub with a minimum of effort.

MATERIALS

- At the center of this tower is a pressure-treated 4 × 4 post.
- The "branches" are 1 × 1 stakes cut short for the bottom, longer for the middle, and short for the top.

HOW-TO

- Dig a hole at least 3 feet deep. Set the post in the ground and backfill (see page 78).
- Cut the stakes to length and nail them to the post in pairs, with one stake on either side of the post. Start the first set just above the ground and the next set about 6 inches above the ground. Nail the third set 8 to 12 inches above the second at a 90-degree angle to the first two sets. Alternate the orientations of each pair as you work your way up the post.

pole teepee

For a quick, inexpensive support for climbing plants, try building a teepee. Because of their temporary nature, teepees lend themselves to vegetables such as runner beans that may not occupy the same spot from year to year. Growing vegetables on a teepee is a lot of fun for small children, too.

Not only does the structure put the veggies at a convenient height for harvesting, but the foliage creates a hideaway under the poles.

MATERIALS

- You'll need three poles, each 1½ to 2 inches in diameter.
- Use several feet of polyester rope or 15-gauge galvanized steel wire to hold the teepee top together.

HOW-TO

- Bind the poles together about 12 to 18 inches from the top ends, making sure the bottoms are aligned.
- Carefully stand the teepee up and spread the poles apart to form a stable base.
- If the teepee seems unstable, anchor the legs. Either bury the ends a short distance in the ground or drill a hole through the bottom of each leg and use rebar to spike the leg in place (see page 83).

garland teepee

It's easy to dress up the basic teepee trellis. This variation uses garlands of grape vine at top, middle, and bottom.

MATERIALS

- For each teepee, you'll need six 1- to 1½-inch-diameter poles, secured with 15-gauge galvanized steel wire.
- For the festive wrapping that makes these teepees stand out, look for grape vine at a craft store.

HOW-TO

- Bind the six poles together 12 to 18 inches from the top with steel wire.
- Once the teepees are in place with their legs spread, wrap grape vine around the top juncture, partway down, and near the bottom. Secure it with steel wire as unobtrusively as possible.

garden focal point

This elegant variation on the humble teepee uses bamboo to memorable effect. The shiny red ball is an optional touch!

MATERIALS

- The teepee's main uprights are 1-inch-diameter bamboo rods.
- The spiral pieces are split bamboo, which is much more flexible than whole pieces.
- Look for bamboo at garden centers, or order it from a garden catalog or online source.

HOW-TO

- Bind the uprights together about 1 to 2 feet from the top, using 15-gauge galvanized steel wire. Spread them out to form the teepee.
- Attach the spiraling pieces by nailing them to the uprights. Predrill the holes to make hammering onto the flexible structure easier.

screen trellis

Whether you are trying to restrict access to your property, provide a visual shield from the rest of the neighborhood, or simply create a more intimate space within your garden, a screen trellis makes a great substitute for a fence. While such a screen is not quite as solid as a true privacy fence, it is also not nearly as obtrusive. And with the right choice of plants covering its surface, the results can be truly spectacular.

The quantities listed on the facing page are for a single screen-trellis section 8 feet wide and 6 feet tall. Build as many sections as you need to create the length of barrier you desire for your situation.

ASSEMBLY INSTRUCTIONS

Start by making the trellis grid. The grid pieces are joined at each overlap with a joint called a half lap, in which half the thickness of each piece is removed to create two notches that fit together. Because there are so many of these notches to make, it's easiest to gang-cut the pieces, as shown in Step 1.

Lap joints add a lot of strength and help keep the grid spacing even. However, they can be challenging for an inexperienced woodworker. As an alternative, you can simply glue and nail the grid pieces together. If you choose this approach, you'll need to cut some filler pieces to go around the grid edges.

1 Notch the Slats

Line up eleven 1 by 2 slats side by side, as shown. Butt one end of the array against a wall or other straight surface to keep the pieces aligned. (If the slats are warped and don't sit neatly side by side, you can gently clamp them together with a bar clamp.) Mark the notch locations across all the pieces, starting 6 inches from the ends touching the wall and spacing them 6 inches apart. All notches should be 1½ inches wide. Set the blade on your circular saw to make a cut ⅜ inch deep. Make a series of repeated cuts across each notch, then clean up the notches with a chisel as necessary. Notch the second set of eleven slats the same way.

2 Cut the Grid to Size

Draw a 6-foot by 8-foot rectangle on the floor with chalk to establish the size of the grid. Place one set of slats diagonally within the rectangle, notches up. Crisscross the second set of slats on top, engaging the half-lap joints. You'll need to cut six of the slats into two pieces each to make the shorter grid pieces at the corners. Mark and cut all the slats so the grid fits within the rectangle.

3 Attach the Crosspieces

Separate the slats long enough to put a dab of glue within each half lap. Reassemble the grid and put bricks or cement blocks on top to serve as clamps while the glue sets. (If you wish, secure the joints with short ring-shank nails.) When the glue is dry, screw the top and bottom crosspieces to the slats.

4 Mount the Grid to the Posts

Dig holes and set the posts (see page 78). If you need to cut the posts, do it before you set them in the ground permanently. Have a helper hold the grid in position against the posts, and screw the grid in place. Cut 1 by 4 cover boards to fit over the ends of the slats between the upper and lower crosspieces. Screw the cover boards in place. Prime and paint the unit.

SHOPPING LIST

- Twenty-four 8' 1 × 2s for:
  Twenty-two diagonal slats
  Top crosspiece
  Bottom crosspiece
- Two 10' 4 × 4 posts
- Two 6' 1 × 4s for cover boards
- One pound of #8 × 2" rust-resistant screws
- Weatherproof glue
- Exterior primer and paint

arbor projects

IN MANY WAYS, AN ARBOR IS SIMPLY A THREE-DIMENSIONAL TRELLIS.

Because arbors tend to be larger than trellises and involve more pieces, they generally require more work to build—but add that much more to your landscape. ■ *Arbors involve some additional components, too. In the following pages, you'll encounter ratters, beams, and decorative overhead slats. You'll also discover that building an arbor is similar to building a very small, simple house. Like a house carpenter, you will come to rely on the three basic standards of construction: plumb, square, and level. Depending on your project, you may even need to recall a little high school geometry to help you with the layout. But don't let that stop you. These are skills that are easily mastered.* ■ *The arbors included here represent a wide selection of design possibilities. Build them as presented, modify the plans, or mix and match design elements to come up with the arbor best suited to your garden.*

pathway arbor

At the entrance to a path or at a break in a stone wall, this elegant but simple arbor will lend visual interest to your garden landscape. Its lattice side panels provide ample footholds for delicate climbing plants such as morning glories, while its rafters are stout enough for more robust vines such as wisteria.

ASSEMBLY INSTRUCTIONS

Because this arbor has its feet sunk deep in the ground, the wood you use for the posts should be appropriate for ground contact. In most cases, this means you'll want to choose some kind of pressure-treated lumber. If you intend to paint your arbor, you can use untreated stock for the upper parts. Try to find the straightest, most knot-free material you can for the best appearance and ease of construction.

As described here, the arbor is about 48 inches wide. For a path of a different width, change the rafter length as needed.

EXPLODED VIEW

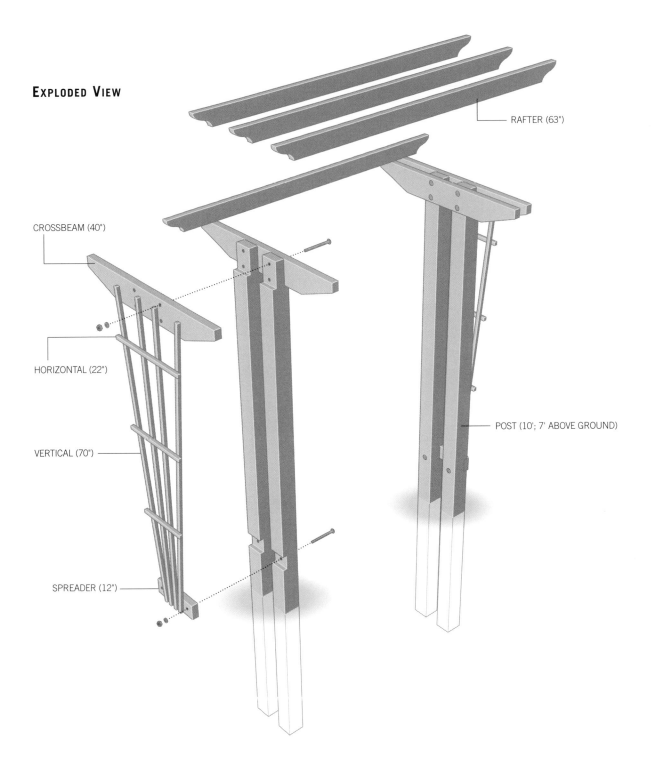

RAFTER (63")

CROSSBEAM (40")

HORIZONTAL (22")

VERTICAL (70")

SPREADER (12")

POST (10'; 7' ABOVE GROUND)

SHOPPING LIST

- Four 10' 4 × 4 posts
- Two 8' 2 × 6s for four crossbeams
- Two 12' 2 × 4s for:
  Two spreaders
  Four rafters

- Eight 8' 1 × 1s for:
  Eight verticals
  Six horizontals
- Twelve ¼-20 × 5" galvanized carriage bolts with washers and nuts

- One pound of #10 × 3" rust-resistant screws
- One pound of #8 × 2" rust-resistant screws
- One pound of #6 × 1¼" rust-resistant screws
- Exterior primer and paint

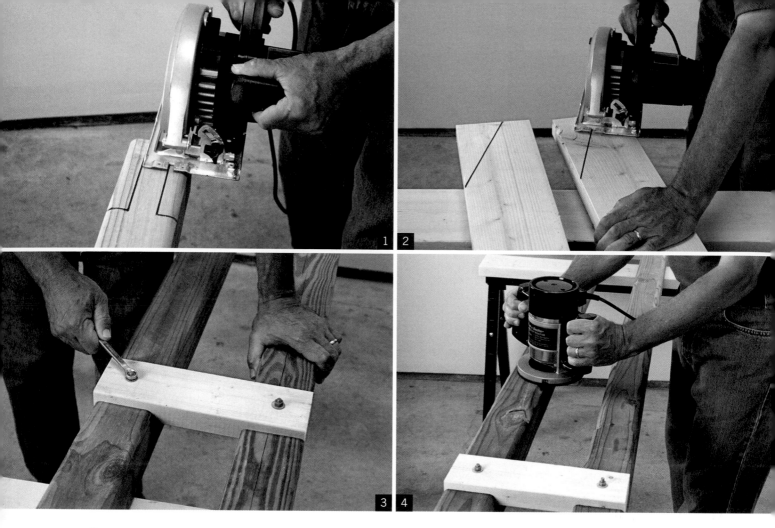

1 Notch the Posts

Start by cutting notches in the posts for the crossbeams and spreaders. Set your circular saw to make a 1-inch-deep cut. For the notches at the top of the posts, make a single cut across the post to establish the shoulder. Then set the saw for the maximum cut depth, and cut in from the end on both sides of the post to free the waste. After you make the end cuts, the waste will be held in place by a small triangle of material. Break the waste free, then clean up the surface with a chisel. Mark for the notches for the spreaders so that the notch bottom is approximately 72 inches from the post top. To cut, make a series of 1-inch-deep cuts across the post, then cut away any waste with a chisel.

2 Cut Crossbeams and Spreaders

Cut the crossbeams and spreaders to length. (Cut one spreader from each 2 by 4; if you cut both spreaders from a single 2 by 4, the remaining piece won't be long enough for two rafters.) Lay out angled cuts at both ends of the crossbeams. These cuts should leave a 2-inch flat surface at the end and extend about 8 inches along the beam. Make the cuts with your circular saw.

3 Assemble the End Frames

Fasten the crossbeams and spreaders to the posts with 5-inch carriage bolts. Put the bolt heads on the inside of the arbor so the protruding ends will point out, away from the path.

4 Chamfer the Corners

As a decorative touch, chamfer all four corners of each post with a chamfering bit in a router. The chamfers should start about 6 inches above the spreaders and end about 6 inches below the crossbeams. Not only will the chamfers dress up the posts, they will make them a bit friendlier by removing the sharp corners—an especially nice touch if your garden is frequented by youngsters.

5 Seat the Posts

Dig a 3-foot-deep hole at each side of the path, wide enough to accommodate both posts. Drop the assembled post-and-beam units in the holes and prop them in place so they are plumb (vertical). Check to make sure the tops of the crossbeams are level with each other; dig one of the holes a little deeper if necessary to make things even. Backfill the holes (see page 78), checking periodically to make sure the posts are still plumb.

6 Add the Rafters

Cut the rafters to length, then lay out decorative cuts on the ends; the exact shape is not important. Make the cuts with a jigsaw. Position the rafters on top of the arbor, with the outer rafters 2 inches in from the crossbeams ends and the interior rafters spaced 10 inches apart. Screw the rafters in place with 3-inch screws angled down through the sides into the crossbeams, predrilling the holes to avoid splitting the wood.

7 Install the Lattice Pieces

Cut the verticals to length. Fasten them to each side of the arbor in a fanlike configuration, using 2-inch screws. Cut the horizontals to length and screw them to the verticals with 1¼-inch screws, spacing the horizontals about 18 inches apart. (Predrill all screw holes.) Prime and paint the entire arbor.

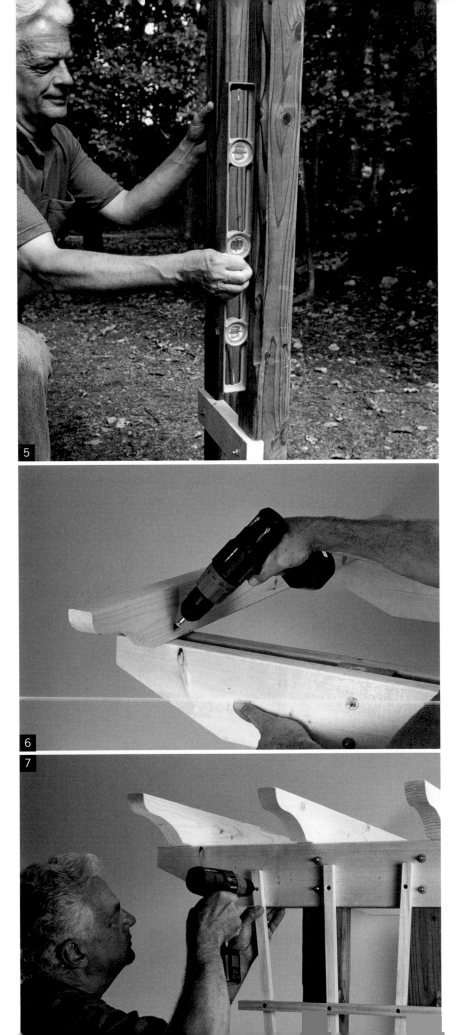

ANCHORING POSTS

When it comes to anchoring trellises and especially arbors (which tend to be bigger and bulkier), you have a number of options. The choice depends on the materials you're using and your local soil conditions, as well as on your personal preferences.

If you are using nontreated lumber, it is best to keep your project away from the ground. Even rot-resistant woods such as cedar and redwood will quickly succumb to the elements if they are left in contact with the soil. Instead, your best bet is to anchor the posts to concrete piers that have been poured in place (see below left).

If you are using pressure-treated lumber, you can set the posts directly into the ground. Try to find posts rated for in-ground use, which means they have a higher concentration of preservative than those with a lesser rating. How deep to set them depends on your local weather conditions and the type of structure you're building. In cold-winter regions, set the posts at or below the frost line—the maximum depth the frost reaches—to avoid having them shift when the ground freezes. This is more important with a structure such as a pergola than it is with a simple trellis. Also, if your project lacks adequate structural bracing, you can compensate by setting the posts at least 3 feet deep.

How to backfill the holes is also an issue to consider. In well-drained soil, it's usually enough simply to fill in around the post with soil, tamping it down well as you go. In sandy soil, you may want to pour a concrete pad under the post and then add a concrete collar where the post meets the surface (see below center). The pad will spread the load under the post, and the collar will help provide lateral support. In poorly drained soil, it's best to backfill with concrete to provide a barrier between the soil and the post. Adding a layer of gravel to the bottom of the hole will also help keep moisture away from the post (see below right). Check with local contractors or landscapers in order to find out what method is typically used in your area.

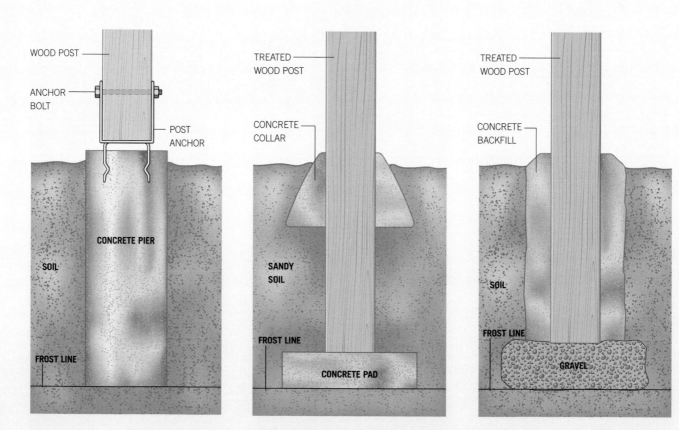

CONCRETE PIER

WOOD POST

ANCHOR BOLT

POST ANCHOR

CONCRETE PIER

SOIL

FROST LINE

SANDY SOIL

TREATED WOOD POST

CONCRETE COLLAR

SANDY SOIL

FROST LINE

CONCRETE PAD

POORLY DRAINED SOIL

TREATED WOOD POST

CONCRETE BACKFILL

SOIL

FROST LINE

GRAVEL

rustic gateway

If you take the idea of a trellis built from bent and twisted branches and expand it into a three-dimensional structure, the result is a funky, rustic gateway arbor like the one below. Placed at a gap in a wall or hedge, such an arbor makes a perfect transition from one section of your garden to another.

MATERIALS

- Aside from the four uprights (which should be relatively straight), you can find a place in your gateway for almost any branch, no matter how twisted.
- The key to building a successful arbor from irregular materials is to have a large stockpile from which to make your selections. Cut a lot more than you need, and sort through the pile until you find the perfect pieces.

HOW-TO

- Start by assembling the two end frames flat on the ground; cut the uprights, then fill in the cross-pieces between them, swapping pieces in and out until you are satisfied with the arrangement.
- When you like how things look, trim the pieces to fit and fasten them together with rust-resistant screws or nails.
- Prop the end frames in place and add crossbeams to form the top of the gateway. Fasten these in place and then add diagonal braces at the corners. Add a series of short "rafters" to complete the top.
- Rest the legs of the arbor on flat rocks to keep the wood from direct contact with the ground and help prevent rot.

substantial rustic arbor

While the crisp edges and straight lines of lumberyard materials look good in many gardens, there are times when the formality of dressed lumber may not be the look you want. Rustic materials, whether straight or twisted (as shown on page 79), can increase your design options considerably. If you don't have access to a woodlot from which to cut your materials, call your local municipality or utility company to see if you can follow one of their tree crews to collect the trimmings.

Rustic materials add a special look to any garden structure, but be aware that they may not last as long as pressure-treated or painted lumber would. For the longest-lasting structure, look for wood from trees that are naturally rot-resistant, such as cedar, catalpa, or locust.

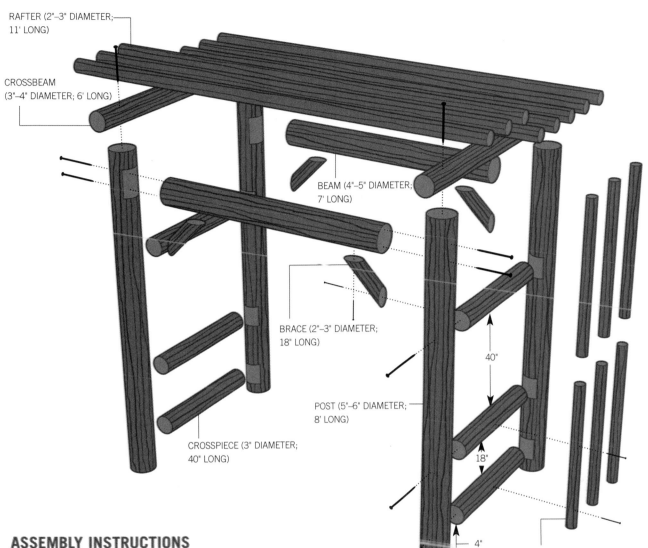

RAFTER (2"–3" DIAMETER; 11' LONG)

CROSSBEAM (3"–4" DIAMETER; 6' LONG)

BEAM (4"–5" DIAMETER; 7' LONG)

BRACE (2"–3" DIAMETER; 18" LONG)

POST (5"–6" DIAMETER; 8' LONG)

CROSSPIECE (3" DIAMETER; 40" LONG)

VERTICAL (1½"–2" DIAMETER; ABOUT 4' LONG)

40"

18"

4"

ASSEMBLY INSTRUCTIONS

Start by gathering the wood for your arbor, cutting some extra pieces so that you'll have a choice of materials to use (and some spare parts). The two end frames are built first, then stood up and joined with the braces and beams. The verticals and rafters complete the structure. As for the site, you'll want a place that is relatively level. Spread gravel or place flat stones where the posts will rest. This will help keep the ends of the posts from immediately starting to rot.

SHOPPING LIST

- Four 8' posts, 5"–6" in diameter
- Six 40" crosspieces, 3" in diameter
- Two 6' crossbeams, 3"–4" in diameter
- Two 7' beams, 4"–5" in diameter
- Four 18" braces, 2"–3" in diameter
- Up to twenty-four 4' verticals, 1½"–2" in diameter
- Eight 11' rafters, 2"–3" in diameter
- Twenty-four 8" galvanized pole barn spikes (may require special order)
- One pound of 16d galvanized nails
- Four 2' pieces of ½" rebar

1 **Lay Out Crosspiece Notches**

The joinery used to assemble this arbor consists of a series of notches cut in various pieces to receive the ends of the adjoining pieces. The notches help locate the pieces and, in some cases, add support to the structure. Start by marking the posts for the notches to receive the crosspieces, spacing the notches as shown in the diagram on page 81. To mark the correct notch width, trace the ends of the crosspieces onto the posts.

2 **Cut the Notches**

Turn each post so the marks for the crosspiece notches are facing up. Make two shallow cuts 1 to 1½ inches deep across the post with a chain saw to mark the top and bottom of each notch. Make a series of matching cuts between these cuts to remove the waste; clean up the notches with a chisel if necessary.

3 **Add Crosspieces and Crossbeams**

Drill pilot holes through the posts into the crosspieces and then spike the crosspieces in place. Notch the posts about 7 feet up from their bottom ends to receive the beams. Also notch the two crossbeams to fit over the tops of the posts. Spike the crossbeams in place on top of the posts.

4 Join the End Frames

With a helper or two, stand the two end frames upright and prop them in position. Set the beams in their notches and spike them in place between the end frames. Miter the ends of the braces at 45 degrees and nail them in place in the corners formed by the posts and the beams. While you can make the miter cuts with a chain saw, you might find it easier to use a power miter saw.

5 Add Verticals

Cut the vertical pieces to length to create whatever opening you want on each side. The arbor as shown on page 80 has a diamond-shaped opening, but feel free to make whatever shape you like. Miter the tops of the top verticals to fit against the crossbeams. Nail the verticals to the crossbeams and to the crosspieces. Spread the rafters out across the crossbeams, spacing them evenly, and nail them in place.

6 Secure the Posts

Position the arbor exactly where you want it. Drill a ½-inch hole at an angle down through each post to ground level. Drive 2-foot lengths of ½-inch rebar through the holes and into the ground to anchor the arbor in place.

WORKING WITH RUSTIC MATERIALS

Building with rustic materials requires a different mind-set than working with traditional building materials does. You'll need to be a little more flexible in terms of size, relative straightness, and sometimes even the way you measure. Because the pieces you will be working with may taper, you need to take this into consideration when you are making a layout or cutting a joint. Try to keep the overall picture in mind rather than getting bogged down with individual measurements that may or may not add up perfectly.

Along with this shift in thinking comes a shift in the tools and materials you'll need. You may use pole barn spikes instead of nails or screws, for example. And while you can cut logs and branches with traditional carpentry tools such as circular saws or reciprocating saws, the best tool for the job is a small chain saw. Just keep in mind that as power saws go, a chain saw is among the most dangerous to operate.

small outdoor room

A garden bench is a great place to rest for a while, but when you put it under an arbor, you have the makings of a truly special place. Even a simple structure can transform a patch of ground into a space that is sheltering and intimate yet very much a part of the environment around it. Such is the power of this small outdoor room.

To build it, you only need to sink four posts in the ground and add some crosspieces, a couple of beams, and a handful of rafters, and you're done—except for whatever finishing touches you choose to add. For these, the arbor shown below makes use of some decorative corner brackets and, for a hint of whimsy, a pair of old window sashes.

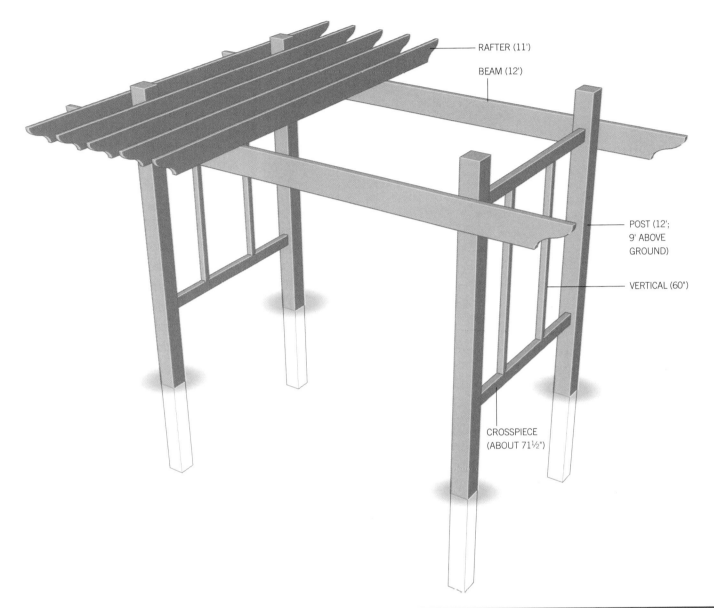

RAFTER (11')

BEAM (12')

POST (12';
9' ABOVE
GROUND)

VERTICAL (60")

CROSSPIECE
(ABOUT 71½")

SHOPPING LIST

- Four 12' 6 × 6 rot-resistant posts
- Two 12' 2 × 8 beams
- Twelve 12' 5/4 × 6s for rafters
- Two 12' 2 × 4s for four crosspieces
- Four 6' 2 × 2s for window-frame verticals
- 16d nails
- Eight ³⁄₈-16 × 8" galvanized carriage bolts with washers and nuts
- Two pounds of #10 × 3" rust-resistant screws
- Old window sashes, about 28" × 24" (optional)
- Decorative braces (optional)
- Exterior stain or primer and paint

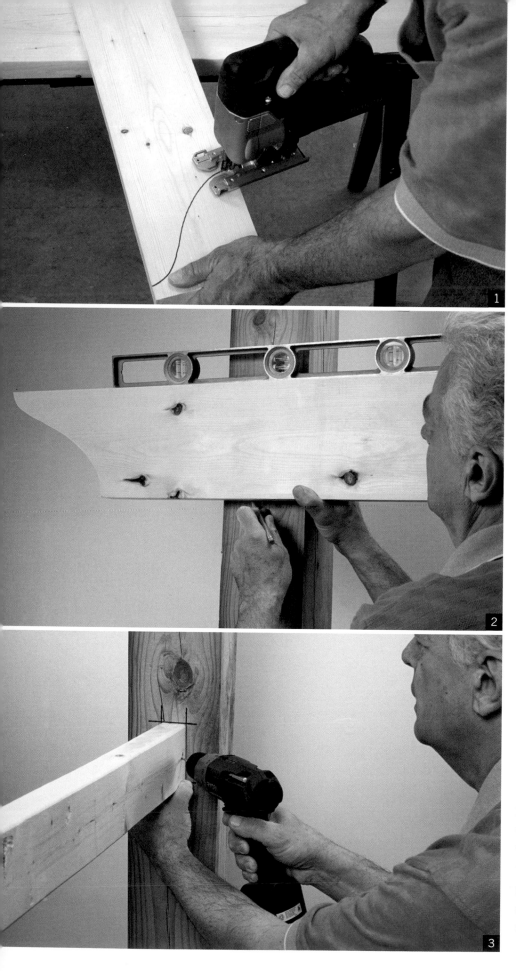

1 Set Posts and Shape Ends

Locate and install the posts (see sidebar on facing page). Then make two cardboard templates for the beam and rafter ends, drawing whatever shape looks good to you. Trace the shapes on the pieces and cut them with a saber saw.

2 Install the Beams

Mark one post 7 feet up from the ground. Have a helper hold the bottom of a beam against the mark while you hold the other end of the beam against a second post. Balance a level on the beam and adjust the beam until it is level, making sure the beam bottom still aligns with your mark on the first post. Mark the second post. Transfer the mark to the other two posts in the same way. Tack the beams in place with 16d nails, then drill holes and install two carriage bolts at each beam end.

3 Install the Crosspieces

Cut the lower crosspieces to fit snugly between the front and back posts 28 inches above the ground; they should be about $71\frac{1}{2}$ inches long, but measure for the exact length. Hold a level on each piece as you mark its location on the posts. Drill three angled $\frac{1}{8}$-inch pilot holes through each end of each crosspiece and into the posts, two from one side and one from the other. Screw the crosspieces in place. Cut the upper crosspieces and install them 60 inches above the lower ones.

4

4 Add the Rafters

Install the rafters on top of the beams. To calculate the spacing, first measure the distance from post to post. Subtract 10 inches to account for the collective thickness of the rafters inside the posts. Divide the result by 9 to determine the spacing between the rafters inside the posts. The two remaining rafters should be spaced the same distance, but outside the posts. Screw the rafters in place, first drilling pilot holes at an angle down through the sides of the rafters and into the beams. If you are installing a window sash, use it as a guide in placing the vertical pieces, which should be securely screwed to the upper and lower crosspieces. The sash can then be attached to the vertical pieces with screws. Once the carpentry is complete, brush on your favorite outdoor finish. If you wish, add decorative braces.

3'

POST

POST

4'

DIAGONAL SHOULD BE 5'

PLACING THE POSTS

While it looks like a big undertaking, building this out-door room really isn't very difficult. The hardest part is locating and setting the posts, but you'll do that first and get it out of the way. The posts should be set in holes that are 3 feet deep, enough to keep things from shifting so the structure won't need much in the way of bracing. Once you have picked your location, setting the first two posts is fairly easy. Start with one side of the structure and position the posts 6 feet apart. Dig the holes and set the posts, making sure they are plumb as you backfill (see page 78).

Locating the other two posts is the tricky part. Working with a helper, use two of the long boards for the arbor to form a big L shape on the ground. Place one board against the outside of the two installed posts, and position the second board so that it laps the first one and extends toward the next planned post. Measuring from the inside corner where the boards intersect (right at the outside corner of one of the set posts), mark the first board at 3 feet and the second board at 4 feet. Then adjust the second board until the distance between the two marks is exactly 5 feet. This means the two boards are square to each other. Locate the third post square to the first two and 8 feet away from one of them. Repeat the process to locate the fourth post. Keep in mind that you're only building a garden structure; it doesn't have to be perfect.

The same 3-4-5 method applies even for a much larger arbor, although you'll need to use stakes and strings (instead of boards) to cover the longer distances.

made for a snooze

Whenever you can get double duty from a piece of garden architecture, you are ahead of the game. And when you couple shade with a hammock... well, that's about as good as it gets. The only drawback will be having to settle disputes over whose turn it is for a nap.

MATERIALS

- Stout 6 × 6 posts form the backbone of this arbor. Use pressure-treated wood or naturally rot-resistant types such as cedar or redwood.
- Top the posts with 2 × 8 crossbeams, 2 × 4 rafters, and 2 × 2 slats.

HOW-TO

- Start by sinking the posts into the ground (see page 78). The holes should be at least 3 feet deep to provide ample support for the hammock and its occupant(s). Be sure to tamp well as you backfill around the posts, or they may shift as you lounge.
- Bolt a pair of crossbeams in place on each post, using a water level or a line level to make sure the second set of crossbeams is even with the first.
- Add the rafters and slats, nailing or screwing them in place.
- To attach the hammock, install an eyebolt on each post.

elegant dining arbor

Elegant scrollwork and a Tudor-style arch embellish this dining arbor, making it seem right at home within a somewhat formal garden setting. The brick base helps keep the area tidy.

MATERIALS

- Because the arbor is painted, you can use standard lumber for the aboveground construction—2 × 2s for the grids, 5/4 stock for the decorative scrollwork. Use pressure-treated lumber or rot-resistant wood for the 6 × 6 posts.
- Select your pieces with care; knots, splits, and missing corners will detract from the crisp lines of this arbor.
- Check out the molding aisle of your local home center for finishing touches such as the turned finial and the trim at the top of the posts.

HOW-TO

- Build the arches in two parts, joining them in the center with a keystone-shaped medallion. Each side of the arch is made from three layers of ¾-inch exterior plywood. Add a strip of molding for definition, and use moldings to help disguise the joints between arches and posts.
- Once the basic frame is erect, build grids to fill in (see page 40).
- Add benches (see pages 102–107) and a table inside.

JOINERY

Most arbor and trellis projects call for simple joints—butt joints where one piece runs into another, miter joints where pieces meet at a corner, and lap joints where two pieces run past each other.

Butt joints have standard 90-degree ends. The square cuts are best made with a miter saw, although you can use a circular saw guided along an angle square (see page 116). The joints are secured with nails or screws.

Miter joints typically are cut at 45-degree angles. Again, a power miter saw is the best tool for the job. (That's how it got its name.) You can also cut these joints with a handsaw and a miter box. Because miter joints are often cut on trim pieces, you'll want to practice before cutting your good stock. However, don't worry about the occasional gap—once your project has been out in the weather, the joints are almost guaranteed to open up somewhat anyway.

Lap joints call for other techniques. Usually when two pieces meet in a lap joint, each is notched to accept the other. When the pieces are of equal thickness, the notches are cut half as deep as the thickness of the material.

If you use a portable circular saw to cut lap joint notches, set the blade depth at half the piece's depth; make two cuts to outline the joint's shoulder, then several more cuts in the "waste area" inside the lines, as shown at right. Use a chisel to remove the waste and to smooth the joint's bottom. Sound tedious? It is! Using a table saw and a dado blade makes the process speedier and more straightforward.

The butt joint is hardly a joint at all—it exists when one piece butts into another.

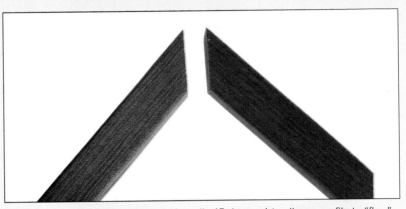

The miter joint involves angled cuts (usually 45 degrees) to allow a profile to "flow" around a corner.

The lap joint allows two pieces of wood to intersect in the same plane. It also helps locate the pieces in relationship to one another.

To cut a lap joint's notch with a circular saw, make a series of repeated saw cuts to clear away most of the waste. Then clean up the notch with a sharp chisel.

gateway arbor

An arched white garden gateway is a piece of classic Americana that speaks of a simpler time, evoking images of Tom Sawyer's whitewashed fence and summertime lemonade stands. This version features a pair of broad, inviting arches resting atop stout 4 by 4 posts. A series of 1 by 4 slats connects the arches, forming a tunnel of sorts and providing support for whatever climbing plants you like. A single hinged gate completes the unit.

Because of the number of angled cuts required, you'll need a power miter saw for this project.

ASSEMBLY INSTRUCTIONS

The most involved part of this project is making the two arches, so that is the place to start. Each arch is made from two layers of short pieces, their ends cut at a 22.5-degree angle and butted together to form the curve. The pieces in the two layers are staggered, much like bricks are laid, to offset and reinforce the joints. There are four arch segments in each outside layer and five in each inside layer. At either end of the arch, the pieces in the inside layer extend to lap with straight sections. In turn, these straight sections lap with the 4 by 4 posts that are sunk into the ground.

EXPLODED VIEW

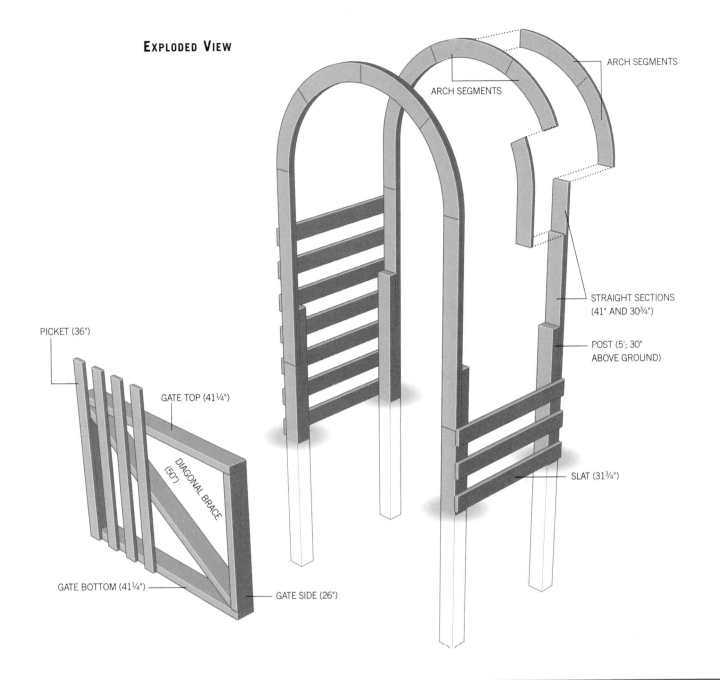

ARCH SEGMENTS

ARCH SEGMENTS

STRAIGHT SECTIONS
(41" AND 30¾")

POST (5'; 30"
ABOVE GROUND)

SLAT (31¾")

PICKET (36")

GATE TOP (41¼")

DIAGONAL BRACE
(50")

GATE BOTTOM (41¼")

GATE SIDE (26")

SHOPPING LIST

- Two 8' 1 × 6s and two 10' 1 × 6s for eighteen arch segments
- Two 6' 1 × 4s for four straight sections (two lengths)
- Two 10' 4 × 4 posts for four posts
- Nine 8' 1 × 4s for twenty-five slats
- One 8' 2 × 4 for gate top and gate bottom
- One 10' 2 × 4 for gate diagonal brace and gate sides

- Three 10' 1 × 3s for eight gate pickets
- One pound of #6 × 1¼" rust-resistant screws
- One pound of #8 × 2" rust-resistant screws
- Twelve #10 × 4" rust-resistant screws
- Gate hinges and latch
- Weatherproof glue
- Exterior wood filler
- Exterior primer and paint

1 Lay Out the Curves

Start by laying out the curve of the arch on a piece of plywood. You may want to paint the plywood white or light gray to make it easy to see your lines. Mark the center along one edge of the plywood and use a pencil tied to a piece of string to draw curves around that point. The radius (the length of the string) is 21 inches for the inside curve and $24\frac{1}{2}$ inches for the outside curve. Divide the arch into four equal sections by marking three lines from the center, at 45, 90, and 135 degrees.

2 Cut the Arch Segments

On the plywood, measure the distance from where the center line intersects the inner curve to where one of the other two lines intersects the same curve. The distance should be about $16\frac{1}{16}$ inches. Cut the arch segments to 21 inches. With your power miter saw set to cut a 22.5-degree angle (many saws have a setting just for this angle), cut both ends of seven arch segments at 22.5 degrees, making the pieces into trapezoids. The short side of each piece should equal the distance you measured between the points on the inner curve on the plywood. On two other pieces, cut only one end at an angle, locating the cut so that the long sides of these pieces match the long sides of the other

pieces. With the nine remaining arch segments, repeat the process for the second arch.

3 Assemble the Arch Layers

For each arch, select four of the double-cut arch segments for the first layer. Measure and mark a center line across each piece. Tape a layer of waxed paper over the plywood layout to keep the arch from sticking to it. Swab weatherproof glue on the ends of the arch pieces and set them in place over the layout, marked side up. Add the other five pieces as a second layer, coating the joining faces with glue and aligning the segment ends of the top layer with the center lines on the first layer. Start with the center piece and work your way out to the ends. The final segments will run past the ends of the first layer. Screw the pieces in place with $1\frac{1}{4}$-inch screws, predrilling the holes to avoid splitting the wood. Drive five screws per segment, two near each end and one in the center. Be sure to drive the heads below the surface so you can fill the holes later.

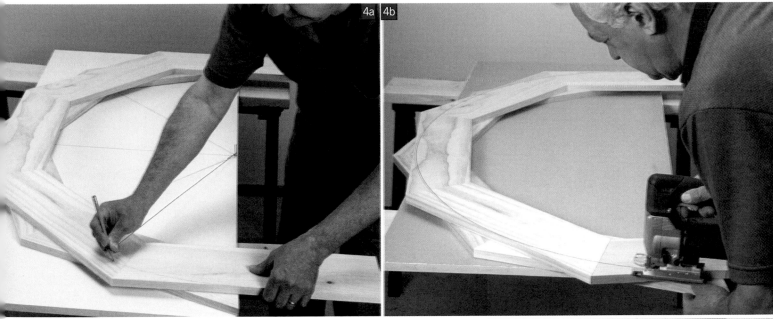

4 Cut the Arches

After the glue dries, draw the curves for the arch on each arch assembly, using a string and pencil as in Step 1. Keep the arch assembly in position on the plywood pattern and use the same center point you used to make the initial layout. Below the bottom edge of the plywood, extend the curve into straight lines where the arches will meet the straight leg sections. Cut out the arches with a jigsaw. Sand the sawed edges.

5 Add the Straight Sections

For each leg on each arch, measure how far the second layer extends past the first layer. Subtract this figure from 41 inches, then cut two pieces that long for the short straight sections of the arch. Cut two other pieces 41 inches long. Each arch should have two long straight pieces and two short ones (see diagram, page 91). Glue and screw one short

piece to each 41-inch piece, using 1¼-inch screws, so that the pieces are flush at one end and along the sides. Glue and screw these straight sections to the arch legs, with the straight sections lapping the arch ends.

6 Notch the Posts

The straight sections of the arches mate with notches in the ends of the 4 by 4 posts. First cut the posts to length. Then make a 1½-inch-deep cut across each post, 12 inches from the end, for the notch shoulder. Lay out the lengthwise cuts to complete the notch on both sides of each 4 by 4. Make these cuts with the blade on your circular saw extended as far as possible. Dig 30-inch holes for the posts. As you get close to the final depth, set the 4 by 4s in place and check that the shoulders are level with one another. Dig a little deeper if necessary to level things out.

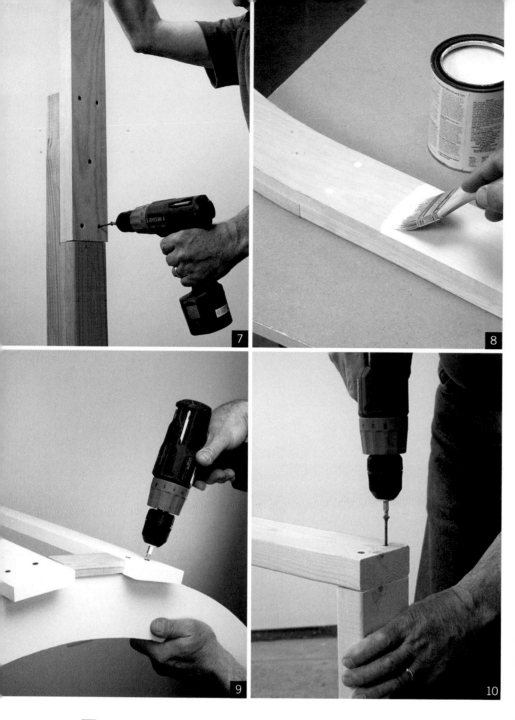

attaching them will help prevent rot; otherwise, there would be bare wood inside each joint, an area that tends to stay damp after a rain. Painting won't prevent moisture from getting into the joints, but it will offer some protection.

9 Attach the Slats

Starting at center top, fasten each slat to the arches with four 2-inch screws (two at each end). Predrill the holes to prevent splitting. Space the slats about 4 inches apart, using two 4-inch spacers cut from scrap lumber. Sandwich the spacers between the slats to maintain equal spacing as you work. Fill the screw holes with wood filler and then give the entire gateway another coat of paint (or two).

10 Build the Gate Frame

With the gateway complete, you can start on the gate itself. The gate consists of a 2 by 4 frame with a diagonal brace to keep it square; a series of pickets completes the assembly. Cut the top and bottom pieces for the gate frame; start with the lengths in the diagram on page 91, but make sure the pieces are about ¾ inch shorter than the distance between the posts. After you cut them, hold the pieces in position and confirm that there is enough clearance for the gate to swing. Cut the gate frame sides and screw the frame together with 4-inch screws.

7 Set Posts and Attach Arches

Brace all four posts in their holes, using the arches as a guide for proper spacing and orienting the notches as shown on page 91. The posts for each arch should be 42 inches apart, and the two pairs of posts should be 23 inches apart from front to back. Glue and screw the arches to the posts with 2-inch screws. When you are satisfied that the posts are in the right places and that the arches are plumb and level, backfill the holes, tamping the soil well (see page 78).

8 Finish the Gateway Frame

Fill the screw holes in the arches and the posts. Prime the arched gateway and apply the first coat of paint. Cut the slats and prime and paint them as well. Priming and painting these pieces before

11 Check for Square

To make sure the gate frame corners are square, measure from one corner of the frame to the opposite corner, then between the other two corners. The two measurements should match. If they don't, apply pressure across whichever diagonal is longer to make the corners square.

12 Install the Brace

With the gate frame squared, mark for the diagonal brace by holding the remaining 2 by 4 piece in place on top of the frame. Mark the ends at an angle to fit inside the frame at both corners. Then make the angled cuts with your power miter saw. Set the brace inside the gate frame and fasten it in place with 2-inch screws.

13 Add the Pickets

Prime and paint the gate frame. Then cut the pickets to length and cut the tops to match the rest of your fence. Prime and paint the pickets, then attach them to the frame with 2-inch screws. Add hinges and hang the gate in the gateway. Complete the job by installing the gate latch.

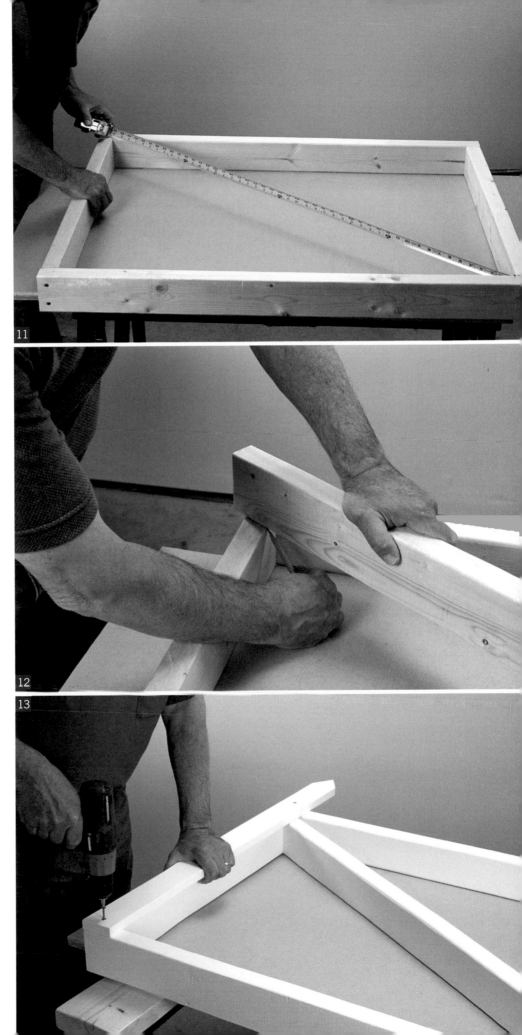

classic arched arbor

This project proves that bigger isn't always better. The small scale and graceful lines of this classic arched-top arbor make it seem right at home in the humblest of gardens or as a hidden treasure in a grander landscape.

MATERIALS

- Because you'll sink the corner posts in the ground, they should be made from pressure-treated 2 × 4s.
- The rest of the straight pieces can be made from regular lumber; primer and paint will protect them from rot. Use 2-foot $^5\!/_4$ × 4s for the crosspieces, $^5\!/_4$ × 8s for the arch platforms, and 1 × 2s for the slats.
- Make the arches from $^3\!/_4$-inch exterior plywood.
- While you can use wooden lattice, vinyl lattice makes the project easier; it doesn't split, and it will never need painting.

HOW-TO

- Start by making the arches from two layers of exterior plywood, as described on pages 114–117. For this project, the inside radius of the arches is 15 inches, the outside radius 22 inches.
- Once you have the arches assembled, use them as spacing guides for sinking the corner posts in the ground. Wait to backfill around the posts, however.
- Nail the two crosspieces that frame the lattice between each pair of corner posts. Also nail the arch platforms to the tops of the posts.
- Nail the arch ends to two crosspieces, and then attach these to the arch platforms.
- Backfill around the posts. Prime and paint all the wood parts, including slats. Then add the slats to span the two arches and fasten the lattice in place.

arbor retreat

What better place to sit and watch the stars come out than on this arbor-topped courting bench? It's freestanding, so you can build it in your garage and then, with the help of a few friends, carry it out to the garden. Over a season or two, you can encourage vines to climb up the lattice panels and across the top to provide a shady retreat on hot summer afternoons.

MATERIALS

- As shown, the bench is built from select heart redwood, but you could easily substitute cedar, fir (with paint), or pressure-treated lumber.
- You could use vinyl lattice instead of wooden lattice.

HOW-TO

- Start by making the two end frames, each consisting of two 4 by 4 posts connected by a lattice panel. Capture the lattice panels between two 1 by 1 strips fastened on the inside of each post.
- Next comes the seat, built of 2 by 4 and 2 by 6 planks and supported by a ladderlike frame of 2 by 6s that is screwed to the insides of the posts. Fasten the angled backrest to 2 by 2 cleats screwed to the posts.
- Once the seat is in place, bolt 2 by 6 crossbeams to the tops of the posts. Finally, cross the beams with 2 by 3 rafters to finish the "roof."

airy outdoor space

Nestled beneath a canopy of taller trees, this light, airy arbor provides a shady destination for an afternoon stroll in the garden. The arbor's wide footprint—about 6 feet by 12 feet—allows the unit to be freestanding atop its brick-paved patio.

MATERIALS

- The corner posts are made from 3 × 3s—not a common size. Have them cut for you, or substitute 4 × 4s for a slightly heavier look.
- Build the gridwork from a mix of 1 × 2s and 1 × 4s.
- The roof structure consists of 2 × 4s that run the length of the arbor, crossed by 2 × 2s.

HOW-TO

- Start by building the two end frames. Use 1 by 4s to connect the posts at the top and about two-thirds of the way down their length. Complete the

rest of the grid with 1 by 2s.
- Add the intermediate posts, connecting them to the main posts with a series of 1 by 2s; use 1 by 4s at the top.
- On the side without a bench, finish the side panels with vertical 1 by 2s.
- Join the two end frames at the top with 2 by 4s spaced 16 inches apart on center.
- Spread the 2 by 2s across the 2 by 4s and attach them 16 inches apart on center.
- Apply primer and paint, and then set a bench or chairs in place.

swingin' arbor

Here's a recipe that can't be beat: take one arbor; mix in a porch swing, a hot summer afternoon, and your favorite book. Then season to taste with a tall glass of ice-cold lemonade. Life doesn't get much better than that.

If this scenario appeals, consider adding a swingin' arbor to your garden. The plan calls for a freestanding arbor made from heavy timbers (so you can swing with your sweetie or your grandchildren) and a commercially made porch swing. The unit is heavy enough that it won't turn over with normal use. However, if young ruffians frequent your garden, you may want to spike the arbor to the ground, just in case (see page 83).

Plan to gather some helpers for the final assembly stages of this project.

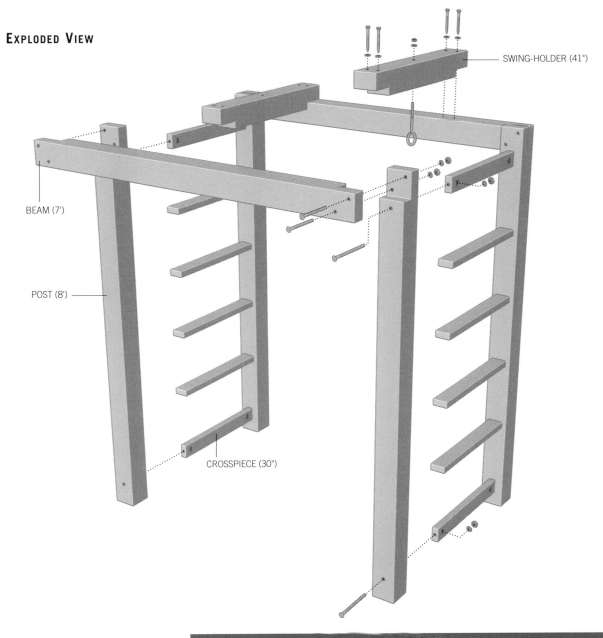

SWING-HOLDER (41")

BEAM (7')

POST (8')

CROSSPIECE (30")

ASSEMBLY INSTRUCTIONS

Building the swingin' arbor requires only basic carpentry skills, but the assembly is more substantial than for a swingless arbor. In order to make sure the arbor doesn't come apart as you swing, the major connections rely on nuts and bolts rather than nails and screws. Start by assembling the two ladderlike units that make up the ends of the arbor.

SHOPPING LIST

- Four 8' 2 × 4s for twelve crosspieces
- Seven 8' 6 × 6 posts for:
  Four posts
  Two beams
  Two swing-holders
- Eight $3/8$-16 × 9" galvanized carriage bolts with nuts and washers
- One pound of 16d galvanized finish nails
- Eight $3/8$-16 × 6" galvanized carriage bolts with nuts and washers
- Eight $3/8$ × 6" galvanized lag screws with washers
- Two $3/8$ × 8" galvanized eyebolts with nuts and lock washers
- Exterior primer and paint
- Porch swing

1 **Prepare Four Crosspieces**
Cut four of the crosspieces as shown in the diagram on page 99. Drill 1-inch holes 4 inches from the ends of each piece, making sure the holes are centered side to side. As soon as the bit pokes through the opposite side, turn the piece over and finish the hole from that side. This will help keep the wood from tearing out at the back of the hole. Make each hole into a D shape by flattening the side closest to the end of the crosspiece, using a file. Next, drill ⅜-inch holes in the ends of the pieces, centering the holes side to side and front to back and extending them all the way into the D-shaped holes.

2 **Attach the Crosspieces**
Drill two ⅜-inch holes through each post, placing one hole 7¼ inches from the top and the other 4¾ inches from the bottom. Both holes should be centered from side to side. Counterbore each hole with a 1-inch bit to a depth of 1 inch to allow room to countersink the bolt heads. Slide 9-inch carriage bolts through the holes and into the holes you have drilled in the crosspieces. Working within the D-shaped holes in the crosspieces, place a washer and nut on the end of each bolt and tighten the nut with a wrench.

3 **Add the Other Crosspieces**
Cut the rest of the crosspieces. Position them between the posts, spaced about 15 inches apart. While the bolted crosspieces are installed face out, these should be turned and installed edge out. You may find it helpful to cut two 15-inch lengths of scrap lumber to serve as spacers to keep the crosspieces correctly aligned as you install them. Toenail the crosspieces in place by drilling two 3/32-inch pilot holes at an angle down through the face and out the end of each crosspiece and into the post, then driving a nail into each hole. Repeat the process with a single nail driven upward from the bottom side of the crosspiece. To avoid dinging the arbor with your hammer, drive the nail the last little bit using a nailset.

4 Notch the Posts and Beams

To create the corner joints, lay out the notches on the beam ends and the post tops. (Be sure that you mark the correct post ends.) On each piece, the notch's depth should be 2¾ inches (half the thickness of the wood), and its length should be 5½ inches (the width of the adjoining piece). Set your circular saw to cut the notch shoulders 2¾ inches deep. If your saw won't cut that deep, set it as deep as it will go, make the cut, and then finish it with a handsaw. Cut in from the ends of the pieces with a handsaw to complete each notch.

5 Install the Beams

Working with helpers, prop the post-and-crosspiece assemblies upright. Set the first beam in position. Drill a ⅜-inch hole through each joint and bolt the pieces together with 6-inch carriage bolts, washers, and nuts. Set the second beam in place and repeat the process. Double-check to make sure each beam is square to the legs, then drill the second set of carriage-bolt holes and finish bolting the beams and posts together.

6 Add the Swing

Cut the swing-holders to fit on top of the beams. Notch the ends the same way you made the notches in Step 4, but make these notches only 1½ inches deep. Measure carefully to find the center point of each swing-holder.

Drill a ⅜-inch hole through each holder at its center point. Push an eyebolt through the hole and fix it in place with a lock washer and nut. Position the swing-holders on top of the arbor and screw them to the beams with two lag screws at each end. Prime and paint the arbor. Then hang the swing from the eyebolts, priming and painting it if needed.

It's a good idea to check the hardware and framing at the start of each season and tighten any bolts if necessary.

arbor with bench

There could hardly be a person anywhere in the world who doesn't appreciate a nicely situated garden bench. And who can argue with the merits of a vine-covered arbor? When you combine the two, you have the makings of something truly special. Find a secluded corner of your garden and install this arbor-topped seat to create a quiet retreat from the rigors of everyday life.

ASSEMBLY INSTRUCTIONS

Building this bench and arbor combination actually is less complicated than building a stand-alone garden bench. Because the arbor provides the structure, the bench just goes along for the ride—no complex angles or joinery. Bolt and screw a few additional pieces to the arbor (predrilling screw holes to avoid splitting) and—voilà—you'll have a lovely garden bench. Use rot-resistant wood for the posts and bench legs, which come in direct contact with the ground. The rest gets stained, so you can use almost any wood. If you want to pave the arbor floor, do so right after setting the posts. This will give you a hard surface from which to measure.

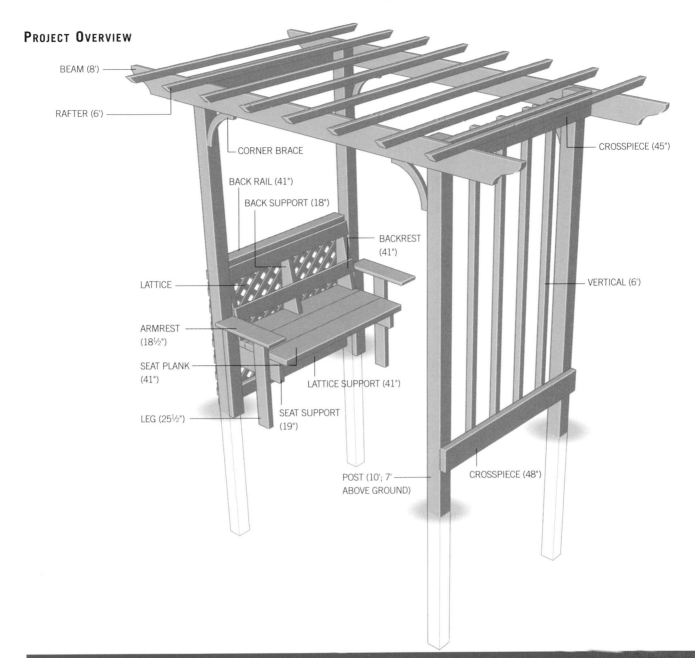

BEAM (8')

RAFTER (6')

CORNER BRACE

BACK RAIL (41")

BACK SUPPORT (18")

LATTICE

ARMREST (18½")

SEAT PLANK (41")

LEG (25½")

SEAT SUPPORT (19")

LATTICE SUPPORT (41")

BACKREST (41")

CROSSPIECE (45")

VERTICAL (6')

POST (10'; 7' ABOVE GROUND)

CROSSPIECE (48")

SHOPPING LIST

- Four 10' 4 × 4 posts
- Two 8' 2 × 6 beams
- One 12' 2 × 6 for three crosspieces
- One 8' 2 × 6 for:
  Two seat supports
  Three back supports
- Two 8' 2 × 4s for:
  Four bench legs
  One back rail
  One lattice support
- One 12' 2 × 8 for three seat planks

- One 8' 1 × 4 for two backrests
- One 4' 1 × 6 for two armrests
- Twelve 6' 2 × 2s for:
  Four verticals
  Eight rafters
- 4' × 4' wooden lattice, cut to 3' × 4'
- Four decorative corner braces
- Eight ¼-20 × 5" galvanized carriage bolts with washers and nuts

- Twelve ¼ × 4" galvanized lag screws with washers
- Four ¼-20 × 6" galvanized carriage bolts with washers and nuts
- Four ¼-20 × 3½" galvanized carriage bolts with washers and nuts
- Three pounds of #10 × 3" rust-resistant screws
- One pound of #6 × ¼" rust-resistant screws
- Semitransparent exterior stain

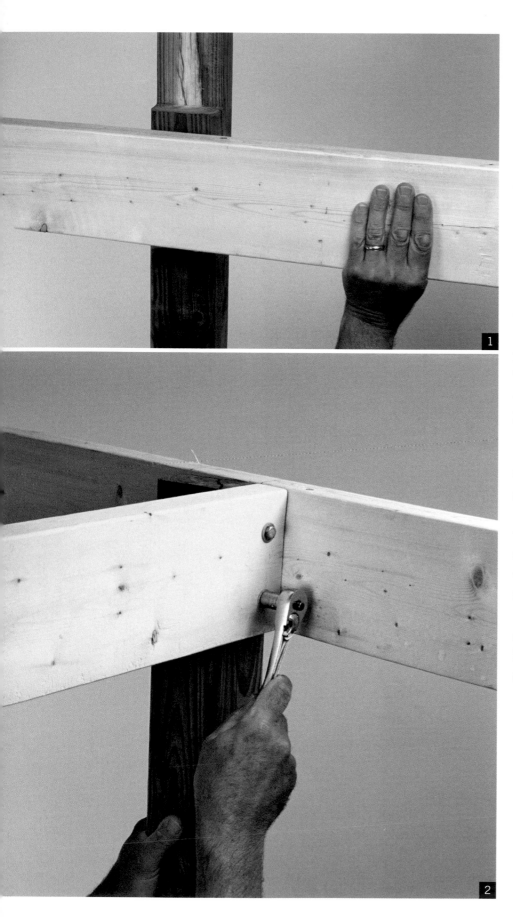

1 Notch for Beams

Start by cutting 5½-inch-long by 1½-inch-deep notches in the tops of the posts, as shown on page 93. Dig four 3-foot-deep holes and set the posts; the rectangle formed by the posts should be 5 feet long and 4 feet wide.(For a method of establishing square corners, see page 87.) Check to make sure the shoulders of the notches are level with one another and that the notches are facing out to the sides. Cut the ends of the 2 by 6 beams to a decorative profile. Seat the beams in the post notches and center them from side to side. Bolt the beams to the posts with 5-inch carriage bolts.

2 Add Crosspieces

Cut the crosspieces to length as shown in the diagram on page 103 and attach them to the posts with 4-inch lag screws, predrilling the holes to avoid splitting the wood. Two crosspieces attach to the tops of the posts; the third (longer) one goes on the end of the arbor opposite from the bench, positioned 12 inches above the ground.

3 Install Seat Supports

Cut the seat supports and back supports to length. Position each seat support beside a post with the top of the support 16½ inches above the ground and one end flush with the outside of the post. Drill a single ¼-inch hole through the post and support, then bolt them together with a 6-inch carriage bolt. Place a level on the seat support and adjust the position of the support as needed; drill a ¼-inch hole and add a second carriage bolt.

4 Install the Legs

Bolt the front legs to the outside of the seat supports with 3½-inch carriage bolts, placing the legs 5½ inches back from the front edges of the seat supports. Screw the back legs to the post with 3-inch screws.

5 Add the Seat

Cut the 2 by 8 into three 41-inch planks for the seat. Set the planks in place on the seat supports so that the back edge of the seat is flush with the outside of the posts. Leave a slight gap between seat planks for drainage. Screw the planks to the supports with 3-inch screws. To make the bench a little friendlier, round the front corners with a jigsaw. Then round the edges with a ½-inch-radius roundover bit in a router.

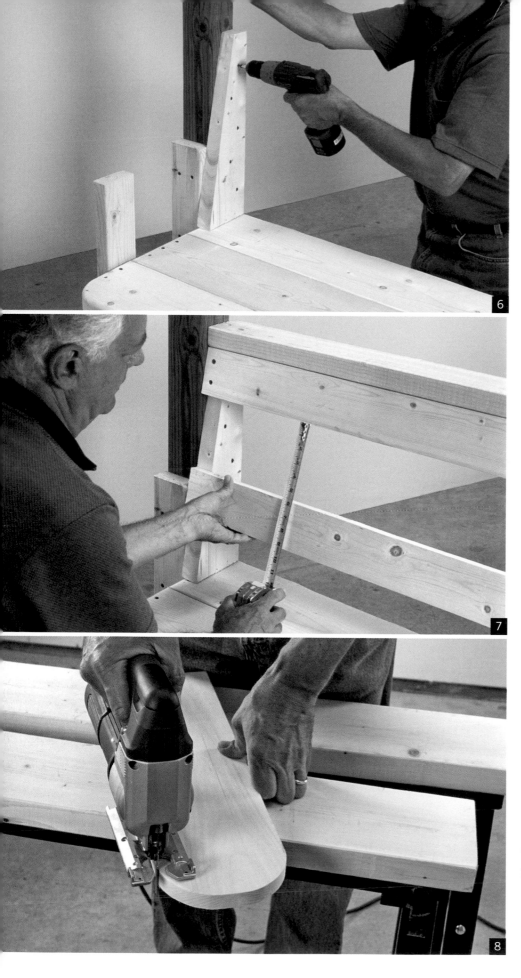

6 Attach Back Supports

Cut the rest of the 2 by 6 you used for the seat supports into three 18-inch pieces for the back supports. Cut the back supports so they taper from 5½ inches at one end to 2 inches at the other. Use 3-inch screws to attach back supports to the posts at each side of the seat, aligning the back edges of the supports with the back edge of the seat. Attach the center back support by driving the screws up through the seat from underneath.

7 Add the Backrests

Cut the back rail and backrests to length. Screw the back rail to the top of the back supports with 3-inch screws. (It will stick out behind the outside of the posts.) Screw the top backrest flush with the top ends of the back supports. Attach the second backrest between the top backrest and the seat.

8 Install the Armrests

Cut the armrests to length and round their front edges with a jigsaw. Sand the rough spots, then round the edges with a ³⁄₈-inch roundover bit in a router. Screw the armrests to the tops of the legs with 3-inch screws, aligning the inside edges of the armrests with the inside faces of the front legs.

9 Frame the Lattice

Cut the lattice support to fit snugly between the two posts that support the bench. Attach it to the posts by driving 3-inch screws at an angle through the face of the lattice support and out its ends—a process known as toe-screwing. Cut the lattice to size to fill the space behind the bench. Then screw the lattice to the arbor, driving 1¼-inch screws into the posts, the lattice support, and the back supports.

10 Finish with Rafters

Cut the ends of the 2 by 2s at an angle for decorative purposes. Although you could do this with a circular saw, it is much faster and easier to make the cuts with a power miter saw. Using 3-inch screws, fasten the first four in place inside the crosspieces as verticals on the side opposite the bench. Screw the remaining eight on top of the beams to serve as rafters. Finish the arbor and bench with a semitransparent stain. Screw the decorative corner braces in place as a finishing touch.

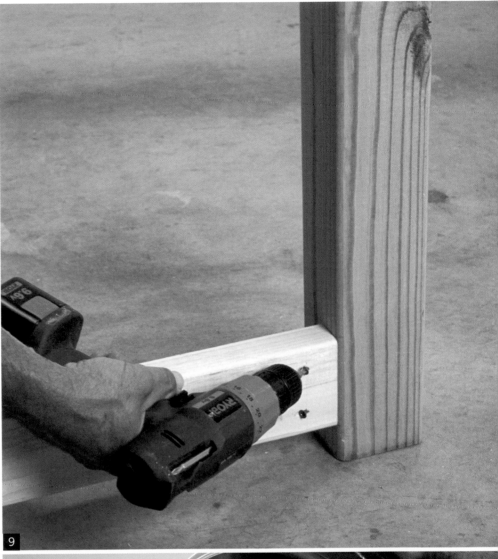

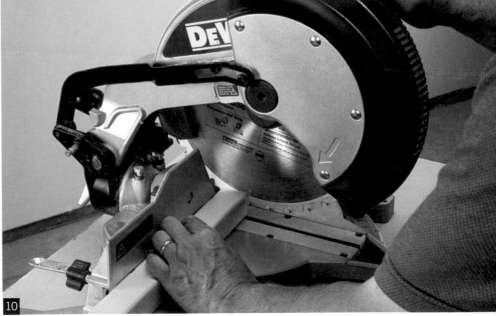

pergola

With its colonnade of columns and classic detailing, this graceful pergola lends an air of formal architecture to a garden. Besides providing support for any number of different climbing plants, a pergola also defines an area within a garden, creating a delightful outdoor living space. Build one adjacent to your house for a seamless transition from indoors to out, or locate it some distance away as a destination for those who venture along your garden paths.

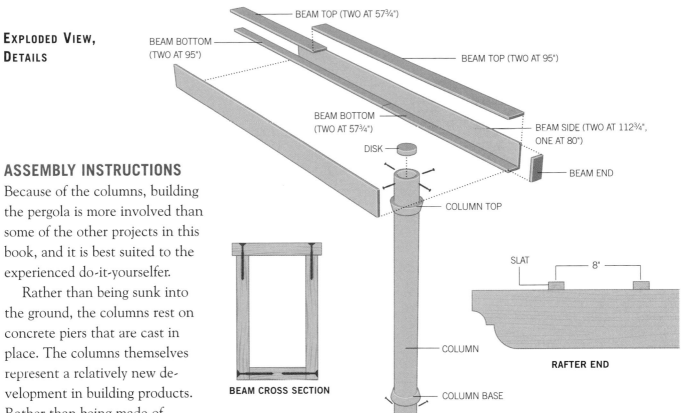

EXPLODED VIEW, DETAILS

BEAM TOP (TWO AT 57¾")

BEAM BOTTOM (TWO AT 95")

BEAM TOP (TWO AT 95")

BEAM BOTTOM (TWO AT 57¾")

BEAM SIDE (TWO AT 112¾", ONE AT 80")

DISK

BEAM END

COLUMN TOP

BEAM CROSS SECTION

SLAT

8"

COLUMN

RAFTER END

COLUMN BASE

DISK

CONCRETE PIER

ASSEMBLY INSTRUCTIONS

Because of the columns, building the pergola is more involved than some of the other projects in this book, and it is best suited to the experienced do-it-yourselfer.

Rather than being sunk into the ground, the columns rest on concrete piers that are cast in place. The columns themselves represent a relatively new development in building products. Rather than being made of wood, which eventually will rot, or stone, which is heavy and expensive, these columns are made from a cast composite polymer resin. The pergola's beams are built up from pieces laid end to end to form each side, top, and bottom.

The plan given here is for a pergola that is 25 feet 5½ inches long and 12 feet wide, including the rafter overhangs. The columns are placed 80 inches apart on center, starting 32¾ inches from the beam ends. ("On center" refers to the spacing between the centers of the columns.) While these dimensions may seem arbitrary, they allow the rafters to be placed exactly 16 inches apart on center. You can vary the dimensions to fit your site, but try to keep the rafter spacing in mind as you plan.

SHOPPING LIST

- One 10' pressure-treated 2 × 8 for sixteen disks
- Eight 10' 1 × 8s and four 8' 1 × 8s for four beam sides (each made of two 112¾" pieces and one 80" piece)
- Four 8' 1 × 6s and four 6' 1 × 6s for two beam tops (each made of two 57¾" pieces and two 95" pieces)
- Four 8' 1 × 4s and four 6' 1 × 4s for two beam bottoms (each made of two 57¾" pieces and two 95" pieces)
- Twenty 12' 2 × 6s for twenty rafters
- Sixteen 10' 1 × 2s and thirty-two 8' 1 × 2s for sixteen slats (each made of three end-to-end pieces)
- Eight 10"-diameter cardboard form tubes
- Thirteen cubic feet of concrete (mix in batches as needed)
- Eight 8' cast composite polymer resin columns
- Eight foam column bases and eight foam column tops
- Eight 8" galvanized anchor bolts with washers and nuts
- Five pounds of #10 × 2½" rust-resistant screws
- Exterior latex caulk, exterior wood filler, and exterior primer and paint

1 Lay Out the Piers

Start by laying out the locations of the holes for the piers. Drive two stakes into the ground and stretch a length of mason's line between them, a few inches off the ground. Stake out a second line 8 feet from the first; measure carefully to make sure the two lines are parallel. Mark the centers of the columns along one of the lines. Push a nail or other marker into the ground at each location. Use a framing square and a straight 8-foot length of wood to transfer the layout to the second line.

2 Form the Piers

Untie the strings, leaving the stakes in place. Dig 12-inch-diameter holes straight down at each pier location. The holes should go below the frost level for your location. (In areas where frost is not an issue, dig the holes at least 2 feet deep so the piers still provide adequate support.) Cut the cardboard tubes about an inch longer than the depth of the holes and drop them into the holes. Restretch the strings and adjust so the centers of the tubes are 80 inches apart. Backfill the holes outside the tubes to hold them in place (see page 78). The tops of the tubes should stick out of the ground an inch or so; adjust them so they are level with one another. Fill the tubes with concrete and set an anchor bolt in the center of each one.

3 Install Base Disks

Cut sixteen disks from the pressure-treated 2 by 8 to fit inside the columns, observing all safety precautions for working with treated wood (see page 46). Try for a tight fit, but don't worry about it too much. Drill holes through eight of the disks, locating the holes so that the disks will be centered over the piers once they are slipped over the bolts. For centered bolts, you can drill centered holes in the disks; for bolts somewhat off-center, adjust the holes accordingly. Slide the disks onto the anchor bolts and fasten each one in place with a washer and nut.

4 Install Top Disks

Fit the second set of disks inside the tops of the columns. Drill eight pilot holes through each column and into its disk, then screw the disk in place with 2½-inch screws. Next, slip the column bases onto the columns. This must be done before you install the columns, since you won't be able to get them on later.

5 Seat the Columns

Set the columns on top of the disks bolted to the piers. Drill eight pilot holes through each column and into its disk, then drive 2½-inch screws through the holes and into the disks to anchor the columns in place. Place the column tops in position around the tops of the columns.

6 Build the Beams

Each beam is a long, hollow construction made from 1-by materials. Cut pieces for the beam sides, tops, and bottoms to the lengths specified on page 109, for a total beam length of 25 feet 5½ inches. Screw the sides to the bottom pieces, alternating lengths so side and bottom joints don't coincide. Inside the hollow beam you have created, screw scrap lumber pieces across the joints in the side pieces, as shown. With a helper, place each beam atop its row of columns and fasten it in place by driving screws down through the beam bottom into the disks in the column tops. Then set the top of the beam in place and screw it to the beam sides. The edges of the top pieces should overlap the sides by about ¼ inch. If you are handy with a router, cut a ¼-inch roundover on the edges of the top to add a nice detail to the beam. Fit 1 by 4 pieces cut from scrap wood into the ends of the beams to close them, screwing them in place after predrilling the holes.

5

6

7 Finish the Columns

Move the column bases and tops into position. Since they are made of foam, you can easily cut away parts as needed to fit over the screw heads. Caulk around the juncture between column and base to fill any gaps; the caulk will also serve as a glue to hold the pieces in place. If necessary, use masking tape to secure the pieces while the caulk sets. Also use the caulk to seal any gaps at the ends of the beams.

8 Cut the Rafters

Make a pattern of a rafter end from a piece of cardboard. The exact shape isn't critical; draw something that you think looks good. Trace the pattern onto the ends of the rafters and cut the rafters with a saber saw. Then install the rafters on top of the pergola, driving screws down through the sides of the rafters and into the beams. Cut a 14½-inch spacer from scrap wood to help position the rafters correctly. Starting and ending flush with beam ends, screw the rafters in place. Then screw the slats on top of them, spaced 8 inches apart on center. For each slat, butt together two 8-foot 1 by 2 pieces and one 10-foot piece; cut the 10-foot piece flush with the final rafter.

9 Prime and Paint

When you have finished construction, sand the rough edges of the wood and fill all the screw holes and other imperfections with exterior filler. Prime the pergola, including the columns, with a high-quality exterior primer, then finish off with two or more coats of exterior top coat. Composite columns take paint readily and look very nice with a plain coat. Alternatively, a little faux-painting can make them look like marble or other stone.

FINISHING TOUCHES

Structural elements that come in contact with soil or are embedded in concrete do not benefit from a finish. But to protect the rest of a structure and preserve its beauty, you'll want to apply a water repellent, a semitransparent or solid-color stain, or paint. Whatever product you choose, try it on a sample board first. And always read labels: some products should not be applied over new wood, and some may require a sealer first.

Water repellents (also called water sealers) help keep wood from warping and cracking. They may be clear or slightly tinted; the clear varieties do not color the wood, instead letting it fade gradually to gray. You can buy either oil- or water-base products, many of which include UV-blockers and mildewcides.

Don't use clear-surface finishes such as spar varnish or polyurethane on outdoor lumber. Besides being expensive, they wear quickly and are difficult to renew.

Available in both water- and oil-base versions, semitransparent stains contain enough pigment to tint the wood's surface with just one coat while still letting the natural grain show through. You'll find traditional grays and wood tones as well as products to "revive" an unpainted structure's natural wood color or dress up pressure-treated wood.

To cover a structure in a solid color, you can choose either stain or paint. Stains for siding or decking are essentially thin paints; they cover the wood grain completely. For custom tints, you can usually mix any paint color you choose into this base.

Paints cover wood with an opaque coat of muted to vibrant color. Because they hide defects so thoroughly, they let you use lower grades of lumber. Most painters recommend a two-step procedure for outdoor structures: first apply an alkyd- or oil-base primer, then follow with one or two top coats of latex enamel. Ideally, the primer should cover all surfaces of the lumber, including the inner faces of built-up posts, beams, or rafters, so it's often best to prime before assembly. Apply top coats after the structure is complete.

Heavy-bodied stains may be either brushed or sprayed on; paint can be applied with a brush, roller, or spray gun. When it comes to complex shapes like lath and lattice, spraying is the easiest way to do the job.

Shown at right, from top to bottom: unfinished redwood; clear water sealer; tinted oil-base repellent; gray semitransparent stain; red solid-color stain.

tunnel arbor

With its soaring arches and precise geometry, this long, tunnel-like arbor will lend an air of formal elegance to your outdoor environment. Build it to lead to one of your garden's visual highlights, or simply add a tunnel to one of your walkways as an enticing way to get from one place to another. As your plants grow and cover the framework, a walk through the tunnel will provide an intimate garden experience.

As you might guess from the photograph, a tunnel arbor is not a quick and easy project. But don't let that stop you. Breaking down the project into a number of small steps makes it seem less intimidating, especially if you have some previous woodworking experience.

Two things that make this arbor look so nice are the square edges of the pieces and the geometric precision with which they are assembled. This crisp, clean look comes from using nonstandard lumber sizes. To duplicate the arbor shown here, you'll need a table saw (or, better yet, a table saw and a jointer) to cut the materials to size.

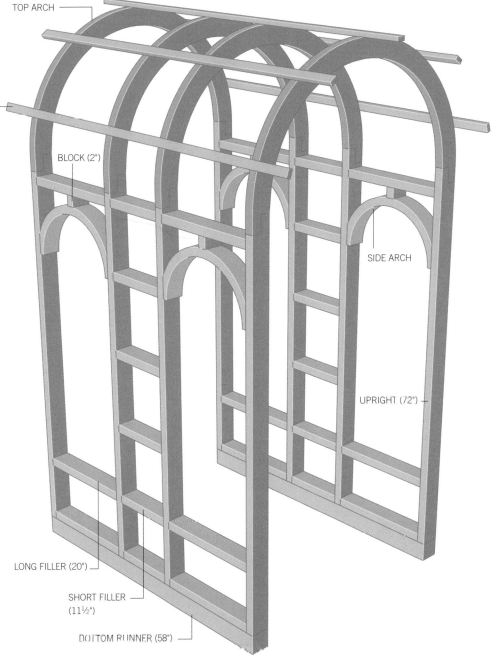

TOP ARCH

SLAT (6')

BLOCK (2")

SIDE ARCH

UPRIGHT (72")

LONG FILLER (20")

SHORT FILLER
(11½")

BOTTOM RUNNER (58")

PROJECT OVERVIEW

ASSEMBLY INSTRUCTIONS

The steps described here are for a 58-inch-long, 4-foot-wide tunnel arbor consisting of four arched side panels (two per side) with a series of filler pieces in between. For a longer arbor, simply add side panels, fillers, and the top pieces and bottom runners to go with them. Each filler and side panel combination will add 35 inches to the length of your tunnel.

Because the arbor is painted, you can use standard lumber for all the framework except the bottom runners; make those from rot-resistant wood, since they will be in direct contact with the ground. Cut the arches from exterior plywood; standard exterior plywood will work, but marine grade is better. The interior layers of marine-grade plywood have no voids, so you won't have to fill any gaps before you paint. Marine plywood costs more, however, and may be harder to find.

Start work on the framework by carefully selecting your 2 by 4s. Look for pieces that are as clear (knot-free) and straight as possible. Avoid pieces with obvious cracks. If necessary, see if your supplier will open a new bundle of 2 by 4s that you can sort through to select the better pieces.

SHOPPING LIST

- One 10' 4 × 4 post for two bottom runners
- Eleven 8' 2 × 4s for:
  Eight uprights
  Twelve long fillers
  Twelve short fillers
  Four blocks
- Two sheets of AC grade exterior plywood
- Five 6' 1 × 2s for slats
- Four 24" pieces of ½" rebar
- Two pounds of #10 × 3½" rust-resistant screws
- Two pounds of #8 × 1½" rust-resistant screws
- One pound of #10 × 2½" rust-resistant screws
- Weatherproof glue
- Exterior wood filler, primer, and paint
- Gravel

115

1 Prepare Site and Materials

Dig a 6-inch-wide, 6-inch-deep trench on each side of your arbor pathway, spacing the trenches 45 inches apart on center and extending them the length of the planned arbor. Fill the trenches with gravel and tamp it well. Cut the arbor's bottom runners and place them on the gravel. Level the runners end to end, make them exactly the same height, and space their outer edges 48 inches apart. Drill through each runner in two places near the ends (or about every 4 feet, for longer arbors) and spike it to the ground with rebar. Next, prepare the 2 by 4s. Standard 2 by 4s are 3½ inches wide; with a table saw, cut ¼ inch off each side to elimi-nate the rounded corners and make the pieces just 3 inches wide. If you have access to a joint-er, use it to remove the saw marks.

2 Cut the Pieces

Cut the narrowed 2 by 4s to length. You'll need eight uprights, twelve long fillers, and twelve short fillers. There should also be enough scrap wood from which to cut the 2-inch blocks. Cut the ends of the pieces as square as possible. A power miter saw will give the best results, but you can also use an angle square as a guide for your circular saw, as shown.

3 Notch the Uprights

Cut a 1½-inch-wide by 3-inch-long notch in the top of each upright. These notches will serve as the attachment points for the arches that span the pathway. Measure carefully and make the cuts as accurately as possible with a jigsaw.

4 Build the Side Panels

Assemble the side panels by screwing the long fillers in place between pairs of uprights, using 3½-inch screws. Position the bot-tom fillers flush with the bottoms of the uprights, the middle fillers 12 inches above the bottom ones, and the top fillers 4½ inches below the tops of the uprights. For consistency, cut a piece of scrap lumber 12 inches long as a spacer to locate the middle fillers above the bottom ones.

5 Cut Side Arches

The side arches are made from four layers of exterior plywood. Cut one piece of plywood 55 inches long. (Save the remaining portion for the top arches.) Draw lines down the plywood lengthwise to establish two 20-inch-wide strips, plus a strip of scrap. Draw a center line down the middle of each strip. Measure $10\frac{3}{4}$ inches from one end to mark the center of the first arch layer. To lay out the inner and outer curves, make a trammel from a piece of wood or a yardstick and two trammel points, setting the points $10\frac{3}{4}$ inches apart for the outside arc and $9\frac{1}{4}$ inches apart for the inside arc. For the center of each subsequent arch layer, measure $6\frac{1}{2}$ inches down the centerline from the previous center point. You should get eight arch layers from each strip. Note that the arch layers will have a flat area on either side. Cut out the arch layers with a jigsaw.

6 Assemble the Side Panels

Glue and screw the side arch pieces together with $1\frac{1}{2}$-inch screws about 3 inches apart, countersinking the screws. Screw the second arch layer to the first layer, the third to the second, and so on. Sand and fill the arches as needed. Screw the blocks to the arches, then position the arches inside the side panels and screw them in place, using $2\frac{1}{2}$-inch screws. Predrill the holes to avoid splitting the plywood.

7 Complete the Sides

Join each set of two side panels by screwing the short fillers in between them, using $3\frac{1}{2}$-inch screws. Position the bottom filler flush with the bottoms of the uprights, and then space all the fillers but the top one 12 inches apart; the top filler should align with the top filler pieces in the side panels. For four of the fillers, you'll need to drill angled holes through the uprights into the filler ends, as the framing will prevent you from drilling directly. Use two screws per joint.

8 Add Top Arches

The top arches are made from two layers of plywood. The outer radius is 24 inches, the inner one 21 inches. After you cut the first arch layer, you may want to trace it to lay out subsequent layers. Glue and screw each pair of arch layers together with $1\frac{1}{2}$-inch screws. Cut $1\frac{1}{2}$-inch-wide by 3-inch-deep notches in each end to match the notches on the uprights. Then prime and paint the arches and sides. Position the arbor sides on the bottom runners, outside edges flush. Drive $2\frac{1}{2}$-inch screws through the bottom fillers into the runners. Screw the top arches to the uprights with $2\frac{1}{2}$-inch screws, predrilling the holes. Screw the slats to the top arches, about $12\frac{1}{4}$ inches apart on center. Fill the screw holes before giving the entire assembly a final coat of paint.

the right plant for your structure

A FRESHLY BUILT TRELLIS OR ARBOR is only half finished until you add a vine. But which plant provides the best complement to your construction? ■ The following pages explore plenty of options, with advice to help you choose the one that's right for you. There are vines of all sizes, including some that retain foliage all year and others that shed their leaves each fall, some that are striking from a distance and others that reward close-up inspection. Some vines have dense foliage that makes a living wall of green, while others form a delicate tracery of trailing streamers. Most have flowers, many of them fragrant. A few bear tasty fruit. ■ Once you've selected the right plant, consult page 122 for information on planting and routine maintenance—training, pruning, and trimming. As a living project, your trellis or arbor will present different faces as the vine grows and matures, ornamenting your landscape more richly with each successive year.

choosing the best vine

Your own taste will guide you in choosing the best adornment for your trellis or arbor. (Alternatively, you can choose the plant first and then design your structure to match it.) But before making your selection, consider the following key issues. Then consult pages 123–127 for information on many popular vines, including some annual possibilities.

Above: Fast-growing Humulus *twines around vertical supports. Left:* Clematis *has coiling leafstalks that attach to both vertical and horizontal trellis members.*

PRIME CONSIDERATIONS

Be sure to choose a vine suited to your local area and climate. It's a good practice to consult the staff of the gardening department or nursery where you buy your vine.

Start by selecting a plant that suits your structure in general scale. For a large arbor, look for a big, fast-growing vine that will provide the coverage you want. (Certain heavy plants, including most climbing roses, should only be used with large, sturdy structures.) For a modest trellis, select a vine with smaller features.

Once you've decided on the right size, consider what sort of climber your arbor or trellis can handle best. Does it provide the right footholds for tendrils or twining, or would such vines need added encouragement?

HOW VINES CLIMB

To know what sort of structure a vine can scale, you need to know just how it climbs. If necessary, you can accommodate the structure to the vine —for example, by adding vertical wires against the sides of an arbor post to support twining or coiling vines.

TWINING

Vines such as honey-suckle (*Lonicera*) send out stems that will coil around any-thing slender, growing upward in the process. In nature, they often wrap around the branches of other plants, which then in effect become living trellises. For upward growth, twiners need wire, string, or doweling.

TWINING STEMS

COILING
Vines like grape (*Vitis*) and sweet pea (*Lathyrus odoratus*) have specialized growths that will wrap around anything handy. Usually forked or branched, these ten-drils either arise from the stem or form part of the leaves. In some vines, such as cat's claw

COILING TENDRILS

(*Macfadyena unguis-cati*), the ten-drils have the ability to hook into rough surfaces. A few vines, like clematis, have coiling leafstalks that behave like tendrils.

Coiling vines need fairly slen-der vertical supports: wire, rope, dowels or rods, or narrow lath. They will also attach readily to horizontal supports, spreading sideways as well as upward.

CLINGING
Clinging vines like ivy (*Hedera*) look terrific on solid masonry, but most are not suited to trellises or arbors. You can't easily guide their growth because these vines have specialized stem growths such as holdfast (suc-tion) discs and aerial rootlets that attach firmly to all but slick surfaces. Thinning and pruning require physically detach-ing them, and the typical dense growth obscures the sup-port structure. A rare exception is crossvine (*Bignonia capreolata*); even so, you'll want to keep a careful eye on where it grows.

CLINGING HOLDFAST DISCS

CLINGING AERIAL ROOTLETS

CLAMBERING
Clambering plants have long, flexible stems with no means of attach-ment, though some have thorns that help them hook their way through other plants. These vines must be tied to their supports, with new ties added as they grow and spread. Climbing roses and bougainvillea are familiar clambering vines.

NO MEANS OF ATTACHMENT

Climbing 'New Dawn' roses create a fragrant living wall behind a rustic bench. Lacking a natural means of attachment, roses must be tied in place.

caring for your plants

The "vertical gardening" needed for trellises and arbors involves much the same methods as you use in the rest of your garden. Think of a vine as a sprawling version of a shrub, root ball and all.

PLANTING AND TRAINING

Most vines are sold in nursery containers that range in size from 4-inch pots to 1-, 2-, and 5-gallon cans. Species vary widely, so make sure to follow the planting and care instructions for your vine.

THE RIGHT TIME TO PLANT Though you can buy vines at any time of year when the soil is not frozen, there are preferred planting times.

Where winters are relatively mild, it's best to plant during winter; this gives roots time to establish themselves before warm weather sets in and the growing season begins. In cold-winter regions, plant as early in spring as you can to give vines as long a cool-weather establishment period as possible.

You can also plant later in spring or in summer, but plants set out in warmer weather must cope with heat stress while trying to establish themselves. Spring- and summer-planted vines usually put on much less growth their first year than do vines planted in the cooler months.

GUIDES AND SUPPORTS During the first several years of the vine's life, you'll need to guide its stems, starting with vertical supports to lead it to the arbor or trellis. For vines that twine or coil, be on the lookout for tangles. If the stems wrap around or cling to each other, untwine them or detach the stems. For a clambering vine with no means of attachment, tie the stems to the trellis or arbor as they lengthen.

Vines often become heavy as they grow; without proper anchoring, mature plants can be dislodged by wind, rain, or their own weight. Make sure to tie all vines—even twiners and coilers— to the structure at strategic points.

Sweet-smelling honeysuckle (Lonicera) forms a rich canopy over a gateway.

Use pruning (top) to develop and maintain a main structure for plants; wires (above) can guide and support them.

PRUNING AND THINNING

No set rule will tell you how much pruning a vine needs. That depends on the plant's age, health, and vigor, and where it's growing. For example, an exuberant, fast-growing wisteria will have to be pruned heavily if it's attached to a modest structure. A large arbor, however, offers plenty of room for expansion, so less pruning and thinning are necessary.

During a vine's formative years, try to develop a structure of climbing stems. Remove growth that competes with the main plant structure, or errant growth that cannot be guided back into place.

For a mature plant, most pruning involves removing dead or weak stems and thinning out excess growth, whether to untangle the plant or to reveal more of the support structure. Some climbing roses require pruning and thinning regardless of age.

a choice of climbers

The plant world offers a vast variety of climbing vines for your trellis or arbor. Here we present a brief guide to some favorites, many of which are available in numerous colors and varieties. Use it to assemble a list of promising options. Then check at your local garden department or nursery for those best suited to your climate and region.

Ampelopsis brevipedunculata

Clematis

ACTINIDIA

STYLE: Twining

CHARACTERISTICS: Tolerates some shade; *A. deliciosa* bears fruit (kiwi); deciduous

SPECIAL NOTES: Requires strong support; depending on species, good for arbors, screens, wall trellises, or fencetop or walltop trellises

AKEBIA quinata
Fiveleaf akebia

STYLE: Twining

CHARACTERISTICS: Fast growing; tolerates some shade; showy flowers in spring; decorative fruit; deciduous to evergreen

SPECIAL NOTES: Creates a mass foliage effect; good for arbors or as backdrop on large wall trellises

Clerodendrum thomsoniae

AMPELOPSIS brevipedunculata
Porcelain berry

STYLE: Coiling (tendrils)

CHARACTERISTICS: Fast growing; tolerates some shade; needs only moderate water; decorative fruit; deciduous

SPECIAL NOTES: Grapelike, heavy; best on sturdy arbors

ARISTOLOCHIA macrophylla
Dutchman's pipe

STYLE: Twining

CHARACTERISTICS: Fast growing; tolerates some shade; deciduous

SPECIAL NOTES: Traditional favorite for thick cover on trellises, screens, fences; avoid in wind-prone areas

BEAUMONTIA grandiflora
Easter lily vine

STYLE: Somewhat twining

CHARACTERISTICS: Tolerates some shade; fragrant, showy flowers in spring and summer; evergreen

SPECIAL NOTES: Requires tying when young; needs sturdy support; use on arbors or very large trellises

BOUGAINVILLEA

STYLE: None; must be tied

CHARACTERISTICS: Showy flowers in spring, summer, and fall; evergreen

SPECIAL NOTES: Use in mild climates on screens, fences, or large arbors

CLEMATIS

STYLE: Coiling (leafstalks)

CHARACTERISTICS: Tolerates some shade; showy flowers in spring, summer, or fall; mostly deciduous

SPECIAL NOTES: Many varieties; better for trellises than arbors

CLERODENDRUM thomsoniae
Bleeding heart glorybower

STYLE: Twining

CHARACTERISTICS: Tolerates some shade; showy flowers in summer; evergreen

SPECIAL NOTES: In warm climates, grow on trellises, posts; in cool climates, use with portable (container) trellises

Clytostoma callistegioides

× Fatshedera lizei

Gelsemium sempervirens

Hardenbergia

CLYTOSTOMA callistegioides
Violet trumpet vine

STYLE: Coiling (tendrils on leaves)

CHARACTERISTICS: Fast growing; tolerates some shade; needs only moderate water; showy flowers in spring and summer; evergreen

SPECIAL NOTES: On arbors, grows long, trailing streamers; on wire trellises, forms solid mass

DISTICTIS
Trumpet vine

STYLE: Coiling (tendrils)

CHARACTERISTICS: Fast growing; tolerates some shade; fragrant showy flowers in spring, summer, and fall; evergreen

SPECIAL NOTES: Use on arbors, large wall trellises, or fencetop or walltop trellises

FALLOPIA

STYLE: Twining

CHARACTERISTICS: Fast growing, rugged; needs only moderate water; showy flowers in spring, summer, and fall; evergreen to deciduous

SPECIAL NOTES: Popular in seaside or arid zones; also use on trellises to conceal ugly features

× FATSHEDERA lizei

STYLE: None; must be tied

CHARACTERISTICS: Tolerates some shade; evergreen

SPECIAL NOTES: Cross of English ivy and Japanese aralia; does not cling, is suitable for trellises

GELSEMIUM sempervirens
Carolina jessamine

STYLE: Twining

CHARACTERISTICS: Tolerates some shade; fragrant, showy flowers in midwinter and early spring; evergreen

SPECIAL NOTES: All parts are toxic if ingested; climbs well on trellises with wires; grows delicate trailing streamers on arbors

HARDENBERGIA

STYLE: Twining

CHARACTERISTICS: Tolerates some shade; showy flowers in winter and spring; evergreen

SPECIAL NOTES: Modest in size; suited to posts, wall trellises, fencetop and walltop trellises, and small arbors

HIBBERTIA scandens
Guinea gold vine

STYLE: Twining

CHARACTERISTICS: Tolerates some shade; long-blooming, showy flowers in spring, summer, and fall; evergreen

SPECIAL NOTES: Popular in mild-winter climates; use on pillars, trellises, and small arbors

HUMULUS lupulus
Common hop

STYLE: Twining

CHARACTERISTICS: Fast growing; deciduous

SPECIAL NOTES: All stems die after frost—remove before spring to allow for new ones

Lonicera

Jasminum

Pandorea

Passiflora

JASMINUM
Jasmine

STYLE: Twining

CHARACTERISTICS: Tolerates some shade; fragrant, showy flowers in winter, spring, or summer; evergreen, semievergreen, or deciduous

SPECIAL NOTES: Many species, easy to grow; produces delicate abundance of foliage on arbors, solid mass on trellises

LAPAGERIA rosea
Chilean bellflower

STYLE: Twining

CHARACTERISTICS: Tolerates some shade; very showy flowers in spring, summer, and fall; evergreen

SPECIAL NOTES: Strikingly elegant; requires sheltered location, well-drained soil amended with organic matter; use on trellises or posts

LONICERA
Honeysuckle

STYLE: Twining

CHARACTERISTICS: Fast growing; tolerates some shade; needs only moderate water; fragrant, showy flowers in spring, summer, and fall; evergreen, semievergreen, or deciduous

SPECIAL NOTES: Most varieties best suited to large arbors; smaller species can be used on trellises and pillars

MACFADYENA unguis-cati
Cat's claw, yellow trumpet vine

STYLE: Coiling (tendrils)

CHARACTERISTICS: Fast growing; tolerates some shade; needs only moderate water; showy flowers in spring; evergreen to deciduous

SPECIAL NOTES: Use to cover patio overheads quickly

MANDEVILLA

STYLE: Twining

CHARACTERISTICS: Tolerates some shade; fragrant, showy flowers in any season, depending on variety; evergreen, semievergreen, or deciduous

SPECIAL NOTES: Requires well-drained, organically enriched soil; *M. laxa* is best for arbors and large trellises, other species for trellises or pillars

PANDOREA

STYLE: Twining

CHARACTERISTICS: Tolerates some shade; needs only moderate water; showy flowers in spring, summer, and fall; evergreen

SPECIAL NOTES: Look for *P. jasminoides* or *P. pandorana*

PASSIFLORA
Passion vine

STYLE: Coiling (tendrils)

CHARACTERISTICS: Fast growing; tolerates some shade; needs only moderate water; showy flowers in spring, summer, or fall; decorative fruit; evergreen, semievergreen, or deciduous

SPECIAL NOTES: Best suited to large arbors; on large trellises, prune and thin often

PODRANEA ricasoliana
Pink trumpet vine

STYLE: Twining

CHARACTERISTICS: Moderate growth; tolerates some shade; needs only moderate water; showy flowers in summer; evergreen to deciduous

Rosa

Solanum

Solandra maxima

Stephanotis floribunda

SPECIAL NOTES: A refined accent on pillars, small arbors, or trellises

PYROSTEGIA venusta
Flame vine

STYLE: Twining and coiling (tendrils)

CHARACTERISTICS: Fast growing; needs only moderate water; showy flowers in fall, winter, and spring; decorative fruit; evergreen

SPECIAL NOTES: Well suited to large trellises or arbors

ROSA
Rose

STYLE: None; must be tied

CHARACTERISTICS: Fast growing; tolerates some shade, depending on variety; fragrant, showy flowers in spring or summer; decorative fruit; evergreen to deciduous

SPECIAL NOTES: Many climbing varieties, suitable for trellises of all sizes; see the Sunset book *Roses*

SOLANDRA maxima
Cup-of-gold vine

STYLE: None; must be tied

CHARACTERISTICS: Fast growing; showy flowers in winter and spring; evergreen

SPECIAL NOTES: Requires shelter from frost and wind; showcase it on arbors, large trellises, or walltop trellises

SOLANUM
Includes potato vine, Costa Rican nightshade, Brazilian nightshade

STYLE: Twining, coiling, or no attachment

CHARACTERISTICS: Showy flowers in spring or summer; other characteristics vary by species; evergreen to deciduous

SPECIAL NOTES: Easy to grow; requires mild climate; most varieties suited to trellises and pillars, large varieties better for arbors

STEPHANOTIS floribunda
Madagascar jasmine

STYLE: Twining

CHARACTERISTICS: Tolerates some shade; fragrant showy flowers in spring and summer; evergreen

SPECIAL NOTES: In frost-free zones, use on obelisks, small arbors, or trellises; in cooler areas, use with portable (container) trellises

TECOMA capensis
Cape honeysuckle

STYLE: None; must be tied

CHARACTERISTICS: Needs only moderate water; showy flowers in summer, fall, and winter; evergreen

SPECIAL NOTES: Tolerates hot summers well; suited to both trellises and arbors

TRACHELOSPERMUM jasminoides
Star jasmine

STYLE: Twining

CHARACTERISTICS: Tolerates some shade; fragrant, showy flowers in spring and summer; evergreen

Vitis

SPECIAL NOTES: Excellent year-round for trellises in prominent garden spots; also use on small arbors or pillars

VITIS
Grape

STYLE: Coiling (tendrils)

CHARACTERISTICS: Fast growing; needs only moderate water; decorative fruit (grapes); deciduous

SPECIAL NOTES: Varieties include table, wine, and ornamental grapes; best on large arbors

WISTERIA

STYLE: Twining

CHARACTERISTICS: Fast growing; tolerates some shade; needs only moderate water; fragrant, showy flowers in winter, spring, and summer; deciduous

SPECIAL NOTES: Very heavy, requires strong support; a showpiece for large arbors; can grow on large, securely attached trellises

The Annual Alternative

Most trellises and arbors are filled with long-lived plants that flourish and mature for years. But there are times when an annual vine is a better choice. You can use an annual to fill in empty spaces on a new trellis or arbor, or to cover up bare stems at the base of an older one. In regions with harsh winters, annual vines provide rich abundance in the warm months without creating unwelcome shade in winter. And, as elsewhere in the garden, annuals offer the fun of choosing a completely different look from year to year.

Certain annual vines are longtime favorites in country or cottage gardens for their abundant color and rapid growth. Gourd vines work well on trellises, as do black-eyed Susan vine *(Thunbergia alata),* orange clock vine *(Thunbergia gregorii),* sweet pea *(Lathyrus odoratus),* and nasturtium *(Tropaeolum majus)*— a favorite for children to plant, with its large seeds, fast growth, and bright flowers. For small arbors, consider cup-and-saucer vine *(Cobaea scandens)* or one of the many varieties of morning glory *(Ipomoea).*

Lathyrus odoratus

Thunbergia alata

Tropaeolum majus

Ipomoea

index

Numbers in **boldface** type refer to photographs. Numbers in *italic* type refer to projects, including photos.